Who Keeps the Dog

Navigating Pet Custody During Divorce

Karis Nafte, CDBC

Publishing

Wenatchee, Washington U.S.A.

Who Keeps the Dog
Navigating Pet Custody During Divorce
Karis Nafte, CDBC

Dogwise Publishing
A Division of Direct Book Service, Inc.
403 South Mission Street, Wenatchee, Washington 98801
1-509-663-9115, 1-800-776-2665
www.dogwisepublishing.com / info@dogwisepublishing.com
© 2024 Karis Nafte, CDBC

Interior: Lindsay Davisson
Cover design: Erika Austin, cover illustration: Lili Chin

Please note the information contained within this document is for educational and entertainment purposes only. All effort has been executed to present accurate, up-to-date, reliable, and complete information. No warranties of any kind are declared or implied. Readers acknowledge that the author is not engaged in the rendering of legal, financial, medical, or professional advice. The content within this book has been derived from various sources. Please consult a licensed professional before attempting any techniques outlined in this book.

Library of Congress Cataloging-in-Publication Data
Names: Nafte, Karis, 1979- author.
Title: Who keeps the dog : navigating pet custody during divorce / Karis Nafte, CDBC.
Description: Wenatchee, Washington : Dogwise Publishing, [2024] | Includes bibliographical references. | Summary: "If your relationship didn't work out as planned and you now must decide what will happen with your dog, this book is written for you. It will help you to put your love for your dog into clear, decisive and positive action whether you have one dog, or four, a Chihuahua or St. Bernard. The information in this book will equip you with knowledge about navigating this difficult decision with tools and"-- Provided by publisher.
Identifiers: LCCN 2024022133 | ISBN 9781617812927 (paperback)
Subjects: LCSH: Dogs--Behavior. | Divorce--Miscellanea. | Dogs--Social aspects. | Pet owners--Psychology. | Pet owners--Family relationships. | Human-animal relationships.
Classification: LCC SF433 .N34 2024 | DDC 636.7/0887--dc23/eng/20240617
LC record available at https://lccn.loc.gov/2024022133

ISBN: 9781617812927   Printed in the U.S.A.

To all my teachers,
human and animal.

Table of Contents

More Praise for

Who Keeps the Dog

Karis Nafte starts this wise, much needed book with a love letter to dogs. By the final chapter, you'll want to write her a love letter. Nafte knows dogs and wants only what's best for them. But the twice-divorced mediation pro also wants what's best for you, including and especially the ability walk away from a difficult chapter in your life with a sense of peace and confidence.
Tammy Lagorce, Contributor to the *New York Times*

Karis Nafte's *Who Keeps the Dog* addresses a critical and often over-looked aspect of divorce. As someone who cherishes my dogs and has seen countless cases where pets are used as pawns in marital conflicts, I find this book to be a compassionate and practical guide. It's an essential resource for anyone facing the difficult decisions surrounding pet custody, ensuring that the needs of our loyal companions are not forgotten.
Susan Guthrie, Leading Family Law Attorney and Mediator, Host of The Divorce & Beyond Podcast and Chair, ABA Section of Dispute Resolution 2024-2025

Karis Nafte is transforming how we think about dogs and divorce. It is easy to miss how much dogs are impacted by breakups and how difficult it can be to make decisions about their future which meet the needs of the pet rather than just the owners. This book offers clear and compassionate advice to dog owners and dog/divorce professionals on how to put dogs (and other pets) at the heart of pet custody discussions.

Drawing on over 30 years of experience as a dog behaviourist and a family mediator, Karis understands dogs and owners, and the difficulties they both face navigating the future after a breakup. Karis helps owners, and those supporting them, understand their dogs so they can find the kindest, most workable pet custody solutions.

Karis is an honest and hopeful guide for anyone facing difficult times and heartbreaking decisions.

This book is a fantastic achievement and I hope it will transform social attitudes around dogs and divorce. Just as we now find it hard to believe that children were once only considered parental property in divorce, Karis is waking us up to the cruelty of seeing dogs as only possessions with no needs of their own.
Jane B Bryan, Professor of Law at University of Warwick, National Mediation Awards 2022 winner

I was enthralled by the book from the first pages, where I was captivated by the idea of the young Karis wandering around with a leash in her pocket in case of finding a stray. The letter to Rover nearly brought tears to my eyes and the wisdom regarding considering the needs of the animal as well (or ahead of) the needs of the humans is truly sage advice.

In an age where many laws do not give animals the attention they deserve as sentient beings it is so vital for separating couples to have the benefit of understanding the impact their separation will have on their beloved pet and for them to be given the opportunity to fully consider what will be in the bests interests of the animal at this difficult time for all concerned.

The book is simultaneously practical and heart-breaking and a must-read for all separating fur parents, regardless of the laws of their country, to help them focus on the welfare of their beloved fur baby.
Jane Libbis, family lawyer, collaborative, lawyer, parenting coordinator

No one ever wants to think that their human relationship will end, but the reality is that 50% marriages end in divorce. Going through a break up or divorce is hard for everyone involved but Karis Nafte gives great advice on how to navigate a break up or divorce so your pet does not suffer. This book helps you look at your dog's individual personality and needs to help decide what is best for them during the break up. She also gives good information on how to make sure you don't lose your pet in a divorce.
Shannon Riley, author of *The Evolution of Dog Training* and founder of Truly Force Free Animal Training

Acknowledgments

To all my clients over these many years. Thank you for allowing me a window into your life and trusting me enough to share your family stories, frustrations, curiosities, hopes, and fears. It was learning from you that lead me to write this book.

To the dogs I have been privileged to work with. Big dogs, small dogs, difficult dogs, easy dogs, intense dogs, and shy dogs. I love you all still wish I could take you all home with me, part of me will always be that little girl with a secret leash in her pocket. Especially to Jasper, Winston, Happy, Tess, Boo, Rango, Hemingway, Jax, Sam, and Bear. Thank you for the time we shared and the things you taught me.

To my earliest cheerleader, Dr Nechama Brodie, who, over a glass of New Years champagne several years ago upon hearing me tell a story about a puppy, a child, and a pair of disagreeing parents looked me square in the eye and said, "you have a book to write." Thank you for the inspiration and support all this time. Sally Cranswick thank you for the many dog walks, and coffees, kindly giving me so much time, encouragement and helping me answer the question of, how do you actually write a book? To Linda Scher, who provided some last precise and helpful feedback on the manuscript. Thank you to Dr. Patricia McConnell and my fellow South African Karin Pineaar for their wise eyes, time and suggested changes.

Lastly to my wonderful family. Thank you all for the encouragement and support from all corners of the globe. To my husband Eytan and my daughter Mae, thank you for the space, the extra meals while I was busy at my computer and for loving me while I was too focused on the book to listen very well. I love you all.

Foreword

by Linda Randall

In *Who Keeps the Dog?* the closing letter from a dog's perspective is a poignant reminder of what really matters: "Don't worry about me. I will continue to be positive and enthusiastic about life. Thank you for loving me enough to make the best plan for me that you can. Yours Gratefully, Rover." This sentiment encapsulates the heart of the book, urging us to put our pets' needs first in times of change.

Divorce, a complex and emotionally charged process, becomes even more so when pets are involved. Karis Nafte, a certified behavior expert and respected divorce mediator, provides a compassionate and practical guide for navigating this difficult terrain.

Nafte emphasizes that dogs are not children nor inert objects, but beings with feelings who deserve a loving and safe life. Her book addresses the emotional pitfalls that often arise during divorce negotiations concerning pets, and she provides clear strategies to prioritize the well-being of the dog. To avoid the three major stumbling blocks in this process: humanizing, weaponizing, and bargaining, she advocates for early and thoughtful decision-making to prevent the dog from becoming a pawn in the divorce proceedings.

The book is filled with practical advice and real-life scenarios that illustrate Nafte's points. Her discussion on how to analyze a dog's needs and behavior, communicate with an ex-partner, and come to a logical conclusion that benefits the dog is particularly precise and honest...and perhaps hard to hear. Her chapter summary questions provide a simple checklist for decision-making, ensuring that readers can apply her advice effectively.

Who Keeps the Dog? is an essential read for anyone involved in a divorce or separation where a dog is part of the family. It is also an invaluable resource for anyone supporting or advising couples through this process. As a veterinarian, I appreciate the timeliness and importance of this book. I highly recommend *Who Keeps the Dog?* to professionals working with dogs, such as veterinarians, dog trainers, and shelter workers, as well as to those working with people going through divorce, including attorneys, financial advisors, educators, psychologists, social workers, and law enforcement. This book is a crucial guide for understanding where to turn for help, how to assess a dog's behavior, and how to navigate the emotional challenges of divorce.

The message is loud and clear: *"Choose for the dog, not for revenge. Choose out of love and respect for the dog."*

Linda Randall, DVM, KPA-CTP, owner, head trainer: One Smart Dog, Seville, OH

Preface

I have loved dogs for as long as I can remember. As a young child it was not possible for me have a dog of my own, but everywhere I went I had a secret leash in my pocket in case I found a dog I could sneak home and smuggle into my bedroom. Attempting to fill the dog shaped void in my life, my parents provided me with a steady supply of animal alternatives with various cats, rabbits, guinea pigs, hamsters, mice, birds and even snakes that I had as pets.

My love of dogs has turned into my career. Since 1996, I have been a professional dog trainer. I am also a Certified Dog Behavior Consultant and an Accredited Mediator. Over the course of my career, I have worked with all manner of dog issues. Anything challenging behavior you can imagine dogs doing, I've probably seen it! I've been fortunate enough to work with thousands of dogs, and their guardians, over the years. Helping people change their dog's behavior requires as much empathy and understanding of people's emotional needs as dogs.

As far as my own story goes, by the age of 29, I had a high level of expertise in the field of dogs and was running a busy dog school and behavior practice. Having effectively resolved all kinds of behavioral problems and worked around the world, my professional life was a place of satisfaction and joy. However, I went through many challenges in my personal life, to put it mildly. I was going through my second divorce, with a toddler and two dogs. The hot humiliation of being a twice-divorced single mom before the age of 30 skewered me to the core of my being. As I write this now, more than ten years into a third and happy marriage, I look back on my life and realize that my earlier relationships taught me many invaluable lessons. When I work with my clients who are navigating their own divorces,

I know how overwhelming, exhausting, confusing and devastating it can be. I also know that the hard times will pass, that there is light at the end of the tunnel, even if the tunnel is a long one.

Over the years, I have witnessed how some of my client's dog's various behavior problems started at the time of a divorce, when a custody decision or plan was made that was not in the dog's best interest. It may have suited the people, for whatever reasons, but it wasn't right for the dog. The signs sometimes show up a few months or even a year after the divorce. Over the years of seeing a recurring theme in my clients of the wrong custody plan or resolution after a divorce, I saw the need for people to be educated about the effect divorce had on dogs. More than just helping dogs through the period of divorce itself, but the ramifications of decisions made about the dog's long-term welfare.

There is a gap in how pet custody is handled, not just from a legal background but from an animal psychology background, to guide the decision-making process so that the best interests of the dog are not ignored. There are emotional realities and legal frameworks, but the very real needs of the dog are not always taken into account. I developed and taught the first pet custody course for divorce pro-fessionals (lawyers, mediators, and judges) to help them understand the effect of custody plans on dogs and how to provide the best guidance concerning animals and divorce.

My decision to work in the world of dogs and divorce is the result of seeing many people who, after separation, were trying to put pieces back together for the sake of their dogs who were suffering from an unfair custody plan. I can guide people through a very confusing and emotional time and help them do what is right for the dog. This has led me to write this book.

This has been an exciting book for me to write as my life's work, and personal experience, come together in these pages. I hope reading these pages is helpful, insightful and shows you a clear path forward as you move through this challenging chapter of your life. If you are interested in the subject as a pet owner or a pet professional and want more information check out my web-site at www.whokeepsthedog.com.

Introduction
"Dear Rover"

When people hire me to help them in a pet custody negotiation, I like to start by giving my clients the following letter to soften and shift something inside them. Pet custody should not be a fight but a fair dialogue for all parties. The narrative of our discussion must move from what is fair for the people to what is best for the dog.

A love letter to your dog

Dear Rover,

Life is going to change for all of us now. Your other guardian and I are having a challenging time which has led to a decision: We are not going to stay together anymore.

You are certainly aware that everything is not okay at home even though you can't really understand why. Maybe we have been shouting, crying or behaving in other unsettling ways. Or maybe we are just not our normal selves.

If there were moments when we were harsher with you than we intended, or we clung to you more than you could handle, I'm sorry for upsetting you.

The reasons behind human emotions can be so complicated, more than a dog can understand. They can overpower us and stop us from thinking properly—even more than a squirrel running in front of your nose!

I want to make a promise to you. I promise to put my own issues aside so that I can make the best decision about the next phase of your life. If I feel angry, despondent, betrayed or guilty, I will not let negative emotions dominate decisions when it comes to you. My priority is to make sure you can live your best life going forward.

I will not use you as a weapon, a pawn for blackmail or imagine that you are like a child. I'm sorry if I forget this sometimes.

One of us may have to say goodbye to you. While this will be confusing for a time, I hope you will adjust to new circumstances if you need to. We will only share you in our lives if you are not troubled by moving between two homes. If having more than one home is too stressful for you, we will not force you to do so.

I promise to love you enough to make the best plan for you that I can. Please know that this hard time will pass. Things will not be like this forever.

Love,

Your Best Friend

About this book

If you are reading this book, your dog is important to you.

Whether you are getting a divorce, ending a partnership, negotiating with your family or neighbors, or encountering any situation where a decision must be made about who will keep the dog, I have written this book to help you make that decision while keeping the dog's best interests at heart.

I tend to speak about dogs primarily, because they are the pets that feature in most custody battles. But what I say also applies to cats, pigs, parrots and all kinds of animals. In this book, I refer to dogs and divorce, but most of the information also relates to other pets whose guardians are ending committed relationships of all kinds.

We need to try to understand what impacts our custody decision has on dogs. Dogs can't put their thoughts and feelings into words, but this book will assist you to discover and interpret what your dog wants and needs you to know.

Emotions such as sadness, depression, anger, fear, guilt, regret and confusion can lead to decision-making based on negative feelings. The turmoil of divorce or the conclusion of any significant relationship can be so overwhelming that those involved cannot keep a clear head. I would not want someone making a decision that would affect my life based on negative impulses, and I'm sure you would not either.

In the story titled *King Solomon Makes a Difficult Decision*, two mothers fighting over a baby approached the wise king. The story proceeds:

> *They argued back and forth in front of Solomon, until he finally said, "Both of you say this live baby is yours. Someone bring me a sword."*

> *A sword was brought, and Solomon ordered, "Cut the baby in half! That way each of you can have a part of him."*

> *The first woman shouted, "Yes, cut him in half. Then we can share him."*

> *"Please don't kill the baby," the second woman screamed. "Your Majesty, I love him very much, but give him to her. Just don't kill him."*

> *Solomon said, "Don't kill the baby." Then he pointed to the second woman, "She is his real mother. Give the baby to her."*

It's easy to make mistakes when stressed or consumed by our pain. But we owe it to our dogs not to allow our complex, tumultuous feelings to determine what happens to them. We need to focus on the dog's situation with clarity and selflessness.

Despite millions of chaotic thoughts that may be flooding your mind right now, you love your dog. Or else you wouldn't have picked up this book.

Divorce is difficult

Divorce is hard on every level, carrying a host of both practical and emotional issues. There is loss and grief, often extremely intense until it becomes a matter of the past. It can take several or many, many months for suffering to give way to energy and happiness again. I know this from my own experience as a divorce mediator;

and twice-divorced, I've been there where it hurts. I've said goodbye to different lives I thought I would live; to loves; and to dogs.

Perhaps you feel that the wisest approach would be to ignore your feelings altogether, but this often leads to overthinking. Neuroscience reveals that we base our decisions on our emotions 95% of the time, and when we suppress emotions, we become more indecisive regardless of how rational we are (Damasio, 1994). Our subconscious plays a much bigger role than many of us are aware of. A lot of our reasons for doing things are actually just justifications for decisions made intuitively. The best approach to decision-making is not to try to exclude emotions but to feel and think; to apply the whole brain to the problem, for its cognitive and affective processes are interdependent.

The fork in the road

There are two troubling paths separating couples can easily go down when negotiating pet custody—troubling, because either way they are not basing their decision on what is best for the dog.

The one side of the track is what I refer to as *humanizing* dogs. This means imagining they have the same psychological needs as children or projecting your emotional experiences onto them instead of being honest about your own feelings or frustrations. For example, insisting on a visitation schedule for the dog, as one would with a child, even if the dog is stressed by a back-and-forth routine. Or saying hurtful things like "The dog doesn't like you anymore," or "The dog dislikes your new partner," when it would be more accurate to say *I* instead of *the dog*.

The other side of the track is where couples simply can't stop *fighting* over the dog. Instead of considering what is fair for the dog, they use the dog to punish or threaten one another; or all communication just turns to an argument, including conversations about the dog. Maybe you have a sensible plan, but when you try to talk to your ex you don't know where to begin or how to prevent the conversation from deteriorating into conflict. Sometimes one or both people are not really ready to let go of the relationship, and they would rather be engaged in drawn-out conflict than quietly close the door on the final scene. The fight is often more about the human beings than the dog who becomes an excuse to keep fighting for fighting's sake, however unconscious the urge may be. You wouldn't want your dog caught in the middle of a stand-off, carrying a burden that is not theirs to bear.

Divorce can be so disturbing that we follow one of these tracks without intending to. Either way, whether humanizing or fighting, we lose sight of the actual dog. This book will guide you along the right path; the third, middle road; along which you consider, with clarity, what is the best choice for the dog.

How this book is organized

This book was written for a diverse audience including, of course, people who are getting a divorce and trying to reach a decision about the custody of the dog. It is also intended for dog trainers and behaviorists who are often consulted by owners to make these decisions. And lastly, lawyers, judges and individuals like me who offer pet mediation services, a field that is growing!

The first three chapters focus on the legal system that people with dogs will face when getting a divorce and how to navigate it. Laws relating to the custody of pets vary widely from state to state and country to country. Information is also included on how to negotiate and recognize that the decision should focus on what is best for the dog.

Chapters 4 through 6 provide you with what you need to know about dogs to make the best possible decision for both you and your dog. Some of this information may be well known to you already, but most people should gain some insights given the wide variety of dogs who may be involved, from purebreds to mixed breeds, adopted from shelters or breeders, and puppies to elderly dogs. This section will ask you both to think long and hard about which arrangement truly benefits the dog the most. And finally, it will ask you to consider if re-homing the dog—giving custody to someone other than you or your ex—is the right thing to do.

Chapters 7 through 11 review all the issues arising from your custody decisions. This may involve a wide range of issues, from the dog becoming stressed about the new circumstances, the challenges if two or more dogs are impacted, and how to navigate shared custody, visitations, children, and how the change can impact you. Chapter 12 provides information regarding hiring professional help if that becomes necessary. Chapter 13 contains a farewell letter to your dog that I hope you will find comforting.

Chapter 14 is written for dog professionals who may be approached by owners for help with their dogs in custody disputes. Trainers and behavioral consultants are telling me that this is becoming a more frequent request. Chapter 15 is designed for those who want to work with pet custody clients offering advice and mediation services.

I have changed the names of the people and their dogs in the stories I tell to illustrate different scenarios, and readers who may recognize themselves need not feel as if I am giving away their secrets as there are really many different people who will identify with each story told. You are not alone in whatever struggles you may face as a dog carer going through change.

My deepest wish is that by reading this book you will be empowered to reach the custody resolution that feels fair and kindest for your dog. May this book bring a sense of calm to the storm of emotions you may be feeling right now and help guide you to a sure, clear place in your heart from which to make decisions about your dog.

Chapter 1
Dogs, Divorce and the Law

When emotional conflict over a dog blinds a couple so much that they cannot make a decision based on what is best for the dog, they may be left with no other option than asking a judge to decide for them. In my opinion, this is one of the harshest things that can happen during a custody dispute. You should not have to leave such a personal decision as who keeps the dog to a judge who, depending on where you live, will be bound by the laws or must make a decision for you without knowing your dog.

This book will help you find the best custody resolution for your dog, or dogs, whether your breakup is new, or it is time to revisit the question with your former partner from long ago. When people are not able to resolve their dog's custody by themselves, inevitably someone else will have to do it for them. The worst-case scenario is that they end up in family court where a judge makes this very personal decision.

This book has four main goals:
1. To help you and your ex find a fair and good resolution for your dog.
2. To leave you and your ex with a sense of peace about the outcome.
3. To keep the decision about your dog's custody in your hands, out of the courtroom, and away from a legal battle.
4. To help owners learn more about their dogs in order to make the best possible custody decisions.

Summary of current laws

Let's start with the bare-bones basics.

What are your legal rights when you get a divorce and have a dog? What happens if you both want to keep the dog?

The way pets are regarded in a courtroom depends on where you live. In most places, dogs and all household pets are regarded as personal property. This means that from the legal perspective a dog is an object, or a possession, owned by only one person. Dogs are not seen as living beings with well-being to consider. Here the ownership of a dog can be proven in court by things like registration paperwork or receipts for purchase. Harsh as it sounds, in the eyes of the law, pets may be no different than a toaster or a piece of art. They are things that belong to only one person. The fact that they are living creatures does not change that. In many places shared custody is not legally possible.

Thankfully, there are a growing number of places where pets or domestic companion animals are defined as legally sentient beings and not personal possessions. France led the way in 2014 by changing its law to regard pets as "living and feeling beings" rather than "movable goods." Portugal and Spain also have introduced progressive pet custody laws.

In the USA in 2016, Alaska became the first state to pass a pet custody law allowing for the well-being of the animal during divorce proceedings; and since then, Illinois, California, New Hampshire, Maine, New York and Washington DC have passed similar laws requiring judges to consider pets' best interests during custody disputes.

Professor Kathy Hessler, who testified before the Alaska legislature in 2017, said that while many worried that passing legislation would create a flood of litigation, instead it facilitated a more peaceful transition for separating families in those few states that have passed statutes.

In Rhode Island, at the time of writing, a law is being introduced to establish custody parameters for pets based on the best interests of the animal (excluding assistance or service animals). In considering sole custody, the court considers:

- Which party owned the animal first or whether they purchased or acquired the animal together following marriage.

- Which party assumed most of the responsibility for tending to the animal's needs including, but not limited to, feeding, walking, grooming and veterinarian visits.

- Which party spent more time regularly with the animal.

- What living arrangement is in the best interest of the animal in question.

- Who presently wants sole possession or ownership and the proximity of the parties to one another to enable shared custody.

- Whether there are children involved in caring for the animal and the nature of their attachment to the animal, including consideration of which parent has custody of the children and whether it is in the best interests of the children to keep the animal in their domicile for care and affection.

In courts where the pet is regarded as more of a family member than personal property, shared custody is a legal possibility. Courts are allowed to make decisions about granting shared or sole custody based on the dog in question and their relationship with their guardians.

According to the new Rhode Island bill, in awarding joint possession of a pet, the court considers:

- How long the animal will stay with each party.

- How veterinary visits and costs shall be handled.

- Who shall be responsible for the basic needs of the animal including, but not limited to food, vet care, toys, pet sitting and day-care expenses while the animal is in each party's home.

- Any additional criteria the court determines relevant to the care and possession of the animal.

At the time of writing, Oklahoma is considering a bill to recognize cats and dogs as sentient rather than inanimate property, and a bill is making its way through the Tennessee legislature after a Nashville man's ex-wife refused to let him see her Maltese Shih Tzu (named Tryp) even though he and the dog had become deeply bonded during the marriage.

In Canada, British Columbia's Family Law Act has had amendments introduced to clarify the law around pets when families separate, requiring consideration of factors such as each person's ability and willingness to care for a pet, the bond a child may have with the pet and the risk of family violence or threat of cruelty. With the changes to these laws, people can look at what is best for the dogs themselves, not as things or as humans but as individual animals with specific needs.

The new rules in British Columbia do not allow for shared custody. According to the Provincial Court of British Columbia when spouses can't agree about their family's companion animal, a judge can order that one spouse will have sole ownership or possession of it. However, the law does not allow a judge to order that spouses share possession or own the animal jointly.

A judge must consider the following to determine who should be awarded custody of the dog:

- the circumstances in which the animal was acquired
- the extent to which each spouse cared for the animal
- any history of family violence
- the risk of family violence
- a spouse's cruelty, or threat of cruelty, toward an animal
- the relationship that a child has with the animal
- the willingness and ability of each spouse to care for the basic needs of the animal
- any other circumstances the court considers relevant

In other places where dogs are treated legally as more than property, shared custody may be an option, and either person can petition for or enter into an agreement allocating sole or joint possession of the dog. Regardless of who originally paid for the dog or settles the dog's bills, the decision about who should keep custody of the dog can be made by factors such as who is the dog bonded to the most, who is the primary caregiver, etc. This means that a family court judge can consider the long-term well-being of a dog during a custody battle.

I use the word *battle* intentionally. By the time you stand before a judge to fight for your dog, the amount of time, money and emotional energy you will have spent will probably leave you feeling as if you have been engaged in combat. In places where pets are regarded as property, when both people can prove with papers and receipts that each owns the animal, costly battles can go on for years.

Establishing ownership

Clarifying who owns a dog is important and is something I often deal with in my pet mediation business/practice. For example, my clients Bella and Tony were in a relationship for four years and Tony's mother, a breeder of Pekingese dogs, gave the couple two puppies from a litter her dog had. No money exchanged hands and the pups were listed under Tony's mom's name as the registered owner. It hadn't occurred to Bella to ask that ownership of the dogs be transferred into her name. When Bella and Tony split up, their dogs were two and three years old respectively and had been raised primarily by Bella.

For lack of a better word, things got ugly when Bella and Tony separated. Tony took both dogs back to his mother one day while Bella was at work. His mother took Tony's side and stated that the dogs were hers.

Bella contacted me absolutely heartbroken, searching for a way to get her dogs back. She could have hired an expensive lawyer, who might have argued that the dogs were a gift, but there was no way to guarantee an outcome and she didn't have the money for a long legal fight. In the end, Bella was left with no choice but to give them up. The story of my client, Bella, and her vengeful ex, Tony, really hits home. Sadly, I have heard countless stories such as these.

When receiving a dog as a gift, adopting from a shelter, purchasing from a breeder or otherwise, make sure that the registration paperwork for the dog is in the correct person's name. Envision the worst-case scenario, the person who gave you the dog tries to claim ownership and take the dog back. Correct paperwork can save tremendous heartache if such a situation should ever happen.

When my clients Munro and Casey divorced, they verbally agreed to share custody of their Golden Retriever. However, without his knowledge or consent, Casey sold the dog back to the breeder shortly before moving to a different country. As the dog was not in Munro's name, he had no other option but mediation, but Casey was not interested. Munro was heartbroken, and I felt so sorry for him.

In another case, Nick's girlfriend Stella moved out with his dog whom he had adopted before he met her. They lived together but never married. When they broke up, Stella decided to keep the dog even though she was legally his. She enlisted the support of her very wealthy parents who never liked Nick in the first place and were thrilled to hear of the breakup. Her parents scooped Stella (and the dog) back into their family home and threw so many legal stumbling blocks Nick's way that he could not afford legal counsel for the full duration of what was an extremely drawn-out case.

At least his dog is happy, Nick says. "My ex hates me, but she loves that dog. He was always content with her, and she can afford to look after him well. I think I must make peace with that. It's not about me or her, in the end."

As we know, and perhaps you know all too well as you are reading this book, relationships don't always work out the way we think they will. If things turn sour or become downright toxic, it is more common than you might think for the owners to use the dog to get back at one another. It isn't unheard of for someone to euthanize a pet just to hurt an ex who is more attached to the pet than they are.

Who does the dog belong to if you got him as a couple?

Most often, the ownership of a dog can be proven by showing which person purchased him, signed the adoption papers, or is registered as the owner through a breed organization. Ownership can also be established or determined by the name that appears on the vet or doggy day-care records, pet medical insurance policies, or microchip contact information. Even if one partner is a better fit for the dog but the other can prove legal ownership, the judge's hands are tied, and she may have no choice but to award custody to the latter as per the law.

Imagine your partner brings home a new puppy. Probably the last thing on your mind is *Who will keep this little guy if we break up?* But here is the reality: if your partner paid for the dog and their name is on the registration papers, the dog is essentially their possession even if you are the better guardian in the long run. This can have disastrous repercussions for dogs and their divorced guardians.

Dogs can be used as a bargaining chip, as a means of emotional blackmail or to viciously hurt exes by keeping their beloved dog from them. Many clients have observed that, in hindsight, there was a fork in the road when the dynamic between them and their exes changed dramatically. At that moment of shift, attitudes changed from being kind and accommodating to suspicious of one another's motives; from then on relatively amicable negotiations about pets became contentious, and there was a fight over the dog.

Advice for couples/partners - sign a petnup!

For yourself in the future, or any friends you have in a relationship who are getting a dog, here is some sound advice. Decide now which of you will take the dog if your relationship ends. Be adult enough to have the conversation about the worst-case scenario of your relationship not lasting. It's best to do this in the beginning while you are happily together and able to agree on what will happen with your dog when presumably you and your partner are getting along well! Signing a petnup, which is a legal document outlining the plan for your dog, will allow you to avoid misunderstandings or retractions later. It's not about trust as much as it is about clarity—when people converse, they may think they are on the same page when they are not. They may recall things differently down the line, and disagreements might flare up that a signed and witnessed document will immediately settle.

After starting my work in pet custody, I developed a petnup contract that is available online. The questions in the petnup are focused on the well-being of the dog more than the personal interests of the people. You can visit my website for my version of a petnup, or else contact a trusted legal professional in your area to help you be thorough, comprehensive, and unequivocal.

Decision making if there is a breakup

For many people, and you may be one of them, nothing matters more than the dog during a breakup. If you can't manage to come to an agreement between the two of you, what are your options?

Hiring a legal representative

If reasonable negotiation with your ex is not possible, if your ex is genuinely not a good owner for your dog, or if your dog is unsafe in their care, then do not hesitate to hire a lawyer and fight for the well-being of your dog.

I advise you to keep all paperwork about your dog in a safe place and maintain a record of communication between you and your ex for future reference. Although judges can make exceptions, the strongest rule of law in places that do not regard animals as more than property will be that the dog goes to the one who bought him or has paid the most for his care over the years.

If, however, you are choosing to hire a lawyer out of fear or anger, I highly recommend you pause and take a breath. The financial and emotional drain from a legal fight is not something I would recommend unless there is no other option.

But the biggest loser in a legal fight could end up being your dog. The stress of being caught in an emotional storm between two people they love most can have devastating consequences. These sorts of legal processes can take months, or years in some cases, and there is no guarantee of the outcome.

Choosing mediation

There are ways—specifically mediation—to secure the future of your dog without the potentially enormous cost in time and money of starting a legal fight that you may not win.

As a mediator, the most effective tool I offer to people trying to figure out pet custody is to shift their focus from their desire for a specific outcome to truly thinking about what is best for the dog. This is not a simple thing to do.

Intense emotions grip our judgment like an octopus holding onto its next meal. Even if we can see the logic of letting our ex keep the dog, the idea of letting go and saying goodbye to the dog might seem impossible to accept. However, when people can find the capacity to see the potential impact of their decisions on the dog, they are more able to make a fair choice, even if it is not what they wanted at the outset.

At each step of the process of separating from your partner and moving forward into your life's next chapter, ask yourself, "Is this right for my dog?"

Summary questions

Can you picture your dog's best interests outside of the context of your relationship?

What positive emotions can you use to make decisions about your dog?

Can you focus both your heart and your mind on your dog instead of yourself when deciding what to do with him or her?

Chapter 2
Is this About You and Your Dog, or You and Your Ex?

As you will see throughout the book, I believe that the decision you make about what happens with your dog after a breakup should be based on what is best for the dog. And I'm sure that you and your former spouse/partner would agree with that. But it is my experience that while one may *think* that they are trying to meet the needs of their dog, humans are complicated, the process of separation and divorce is stressful and emotional, and so sometimes your feelings about your ex can cloud over the needs of the dog.

Self-reflection exercises

I recommend that you use self-reflection to separate your feelings about your ex from your feelings about your dog. Although your dog may remind you of your ex, was once shared by you, and may stand for another life you and your ex once invested in and another future you once hoped for, your dog is a unique, individual creature with a life of its own. If you had not chosen them, someone else would have; your dog would be living elsewhere with other people and probably doing just as well in a completely different place and under different circumstances. As much as your dog was part of the life you both shared, it is also an individual being who deserves to be seen as such. Similarly, you are separate from your dog and whatever circumstances you find yourself in.

Be introspective

You have worth that resides simply in your being you. Try paying attention to the present moment; observe what is without evaluation or criticism; and accept whatever you experience (pain, hurt, doubt, etc.) without becoming attached to it as self-defining.

Regular introspection will help you to refocus on positive thoughts and feelings that will help you make the best sorts of decisions. Instead of searching for answers to why you feel the way you do or why things have happened, look at what has happened and what you feel instead. Ask yourself questions that highlight what you are like and how you think and feel, without self-judgment.

Here are some examples of the questions you can ask yourself:

- Am I getting stressed out by matters that are out of my control?
- What matters are within my control?
- What am I worried about in the future?
- What do I love about my life?
- What do I want to do next?

Don't try to assess your self-worth through the eyes of your dog. Your dog does not see you the way another person would. Your dog does not need you to be perfect, successful, productive and in an ideal state of mind; but they do need you to be predictable and available. It's easy to neglect the dog and their normal routines when life becomes demanding.

Rather than trying to relate to the dog on an emotional level, the most valuable thing you can do is to maintain consistent routines and exercise. Do the activities your dog likes the most like a walk, a game of fetch at the park or maybe a ride in the car, to settle their body and mind when things feel a bit overwhelming.

Stumbling blocks

During separation, three of the largest stumbling blocks to doing what is best for the dog are:

1. Humanizing the dog
2. Weaponizing the dog
3. Bargaining over the dog

In each of the above scenarios, you may lose sight of the interests of the dog, and this can have a negative impact on your ability to come to a rational decision or agreement with your human partner over the future custody of the dog.

Humanizing the dog

Most of us are guilty of anthropomorphizing dogs, and there is nothing wrong with doing so with a sense of humor. However, you should avoid humanizing your dog as if he or she were literally a child. If your dog has become a child substitute in your heart, if you are genuinely upset if someone calls you a dog guardian instead of a dog dad or dog mom, it may be difficult to make a clear-headed decision about custody. If you can't see dogs for what they are, you are less likely to see a dog's needs for what they are. That said, recent research done at the Animal Behavior Society (animalbehaviorsociety. org) suggests that dogs are more like us in their emotional capacity than previously thought. Being anthropomorphic allows us to be empathetic and compassionate towards our dogs, but also can get us into trouble when our own emotional lives become overwhelming, like during a divorce. We do share many of our emotions with dogs, but they are not an extension of ourselves.

If you humanize your dog, you will be inclined to project your own feelings onto your dog such as:

- "The dog does not like your new girlfriend."
- "The dog is mad at me for having an affair."
- "The dog feels guilty that we are breaking up and thinks it's his fault."

These statements indicate you are projecting your own deeper feelings directly onto your dog, almost as if he or she were literally a child. You might hear yourself saying, "I know Rover really wants to live with me," instead of "I really want Rover to live with me."

I am not suggesting that anyone should regard the dog as an object or a lesser living being than a human, quite the opposite. I'm stressing this point because in order to care for our dogs in the best way possible, we must acknowledge our own emotional needs first. Then we can take a deep breath and think about our dogs as individuals, not an extension of ourselves. I'm certain that many dog professionals would argue that dogs are as layered and complicated as we are and that they have as vast a range of emotions—even if it is challenging scientists on how to measure those emotions—as humans do. I recommend the book *Mood Matters* by Karin Pienaar for her excellent research into emotions and animal behavior if you want more detailed information on this subject.

Weaponizing the dog

In the context of this book, I refer to weaponizing the dog not as being overtly violent toward the dog itself, but as a tool to intimidate the ex-partner. Let us discuss what it looks like when someone uses a dog as a threat or as part of a power dynamic. During a divorce, the dog can become yet something else to fight about. Winning the fight over the dog can easily take precedence over the welfare of the dog. Dogs that end up being caught in the fight are the ones I sometimes see months later in need of intervention and behavioral help because they are stressed out by what happened at that time, or the "winner" of the fight was clearly not the person who should have been given custody of the dog.

Probably no one knows you better than your ex. As you are probably aware, divorce can bring out the worst in people. Person A might know that the dog is Person B's Achilles' heel or vulnerability and may use this to wield power over them, push their buttons and set them off, or delay proceedings, and so on. If the issue of the dog is not addressed early, it can hang over everything like a dark cloud and affect broader negotiations. Person B may try to placate Person A by playing nice so that they can win the one and only thing that matters to them—custody of the dog.

In more extreme cases, one person may accuse the other of violence toward the dog. This means someone will have to involve law enforcement or an anti-cruelty organization such as the SPCA. Mediation will not be feasible for this situation unless it is a false accusation. In 37 states in the USA, it is possible to obtain a pet protection order to keep a pet in a place of safety until a divorce is finalized. These laws are incredibly valuable when there is a real risk to a dog (sadly, there are people who will hurt or kill a pet out of revenge during a breakup), but it can be misused if the allegations are false.

Bargaining over the dog

This brings us to bargaining, which is much easier to deal with than weaponizing. Even though this is listed as a stumbling block, I am somewhat relieved if someone tries to bargain over the dog. Bargaining does not need to lead to a fight, it can be an opening to an honest negotiation. If Jean tells Anne, "You can have the pooch if I can have the Porsche," then we know that for Jean the value of the dog can be offset by another item. This is a wonderful direction to explore so that we can find some way that both parties feel okay about what was exchanged for the dog.

There is danger with a bargaining situation, as in the above example. Anne should not give up too much for the dog or be exploited in the exchange. I had a client once who was prepared to give up some treasured art she inherited from her late father to keep her dog. The truth was her ex was being utterly vindictive in asking for the art. He did not want the art as much as he wanted to hurt his ex. I advised her not to give up anything that she might regret later, which thankfully she understood. The bargain should be fair. And it should be made upfront before anything else is resolved, otherwise, the dog can become a bargaining chip with messy, immeasurable value attached.

The mediation process will likely be stressful for a dog

Many a client wants to bring their dog into the mediation sessions I conduct. There is often a desire to show me who the dog loves the most, or because people want me to somehow talk to the dog. I always explain that it isn't necessary for me to see the dog during a mediation session and is likely to cause the dog a lot of stress. As I always emphasize in my work, dogs are often more aware of what is going on than we think.

Let's look at joining a mediation session from a dog's point of view. He will come to a new indoor place he is not familiar with. Both dog's people will likely be acting strange and stressed. There is a new person (me) sitting in the room and everyone will be talking or trying to get the dog to sit next to them. I imagine that dog thinks he is going to a vet or kennel rather than being in a mediation session. Either way, a dog who is stressed is a dog who won't be acting normal, and in those circumstances, the dog can tell me nothing.

During divorce, or any difficult time you may go through, your dog will be tuned into the fact that you are not acting like your normal self. Depending on their breed and individual history, dogs will respond in different ways to a person who is struggling. When I'm having a bad day, my two dogs who are most focused on me tend to have opposite reactions. If I stub my toe and start crying, my dog Jax will disappear. His response to an unhappy person is to sit under the bushes in his favorite part of the garden until things feel normal again. My other dog Sam tries to "help" for lack of a better word. If he sees me crying from a painful toe stub, Sam will do the opposite of giving me space. He will bring me socks or toys. He will sit as close to me as possible, on my lap if I let him, and lick my face. He will bark and bring me his leash (which means "let's go to the park, okay?") Both Sam and Jax are highly sensitive working breed dogs, but their reactions to intense emotion are totally different. The parallels with people are obvious, we all act differently around unhappy people.

Because of the emotional stress the dog is probably experiencing, the way to get a more accurate idea of who the dog is bonded with is by getting a history of the dog, rather than by seeing the dog with the couple for an hour. Then we must find a solution that satisfies both of them because although my primary objective is to do what is best for the dog, the people have to be at peace with their decision, or they won't follow through with the agreement. In a mediation setting, I find that by asking the right questions, people discover the right answers. They may be lost in their own emotions but, with some support and guidance, they reach conclusions that they are more likely to stick to because they came up with them themselves.

Going through separation or divorce, your emotions will inevitably be complicated, layered and difficult. Even amicable divorces will involve feelings of loss and apprehension about the future. No matter how well you handle the event, your dog may be able to sense that there is something different and stressful going on. Some dogs are sensitive to stress in the people they live with.

Ask yourself, "How is my dog responding to the stress in the household? Is my dog actually fine? Or is my dog acting different than normal?"

When people they live with are going through a difficult time, some dogs respond in an effort to calm you or alleviate the tension in the household. Other dogs try to avoid the hard emotions. Like Sam and Jax, dogs will respond differently to a very unhappy or angry person. Some dogs will become playful, trying to snap you out of it by distracting you, bringing you toys, being silly, barking or racing through the house to make you chase them. Other dogs will become low-key, sleep more and or seem to be avoiding you. They may try to be close to you and have more physical contact. If there is more than one dog in the house, they may play more roughly with one another and have mini pseudo-fights, especially if they've heard you shouting and fighting. Dogs with a background of abuse may be terrified by your anger and hide, avoid eye contact and appear nervous; they may even urinate or try to bite you if you come too near to them. When you can see the whites of a dog's eyes, it is usually a sign that they are stressed.

Don't think of change in your dog's behavior as a measure of your capability or associate it with the complexities of your divorce. The dog does not judge you, reflect on the past or worry about the future; they simply react to you and your body language then and there. For those of you who want to learn more about the stress dogs may go through during this process and how to read a stressed dog's body language, more detailed information is provided in Chapter 7.

Summary questions

Do you feel the conversation about the custody of your dog is more about hurting each other than thinking about the wellbeing of your dog?

Is there something that would, in your eyes, be a fair exchange for your dog?

Are you or your ex using the dog for leverage?

Chapter 3
Negotiating Guidelines

Now that we have covered the biases, issues and stumbling blocks relating to their dogs that people may encounter when they decide to split up, let's turn to the guidelines that I have found to be effective in my pet mediation practice when people are ready to negotiate.

During pet custody mediation, I focus on the following six golden rules:

1. Talk about your dog as soon as possible

2. Put the well-being of your dog first

3. Consider shared custody wisely

4. Agree to a trial period for shared custody

5. Be cautious about agreeing to let your ex visit the dog "anytime"

6. Focus on the future in negotiations

Talk about your dog as soon as possible

After your break-up, start talking as soon as possible about what should happen to the dog. Talk about your dog first, not last, during your divorce. For some people, the dog may not seem as important as other factors that need to be sorted out, but even then, it is a good idea to resolve what happens to the dog first, for the dog's sake, and get that out of the way. There are others for whom the subject of the dog is too emotional, or they are reluctant to bring it up because they're afraid of the emotional fallout that may follow.

They may be afraid of losing the dog or fighting over him on top of everything else. The subject can loom, an elephant in the room, casting a shadow over the whole divorce process.

Regardless of why people leave the dog to the end of divorce negotiations, that is when the fight about the dog becomes bigger than it needs to be. The sooner you decide about the dog, the less likely you will be tempted to use the dog as a bargaining chip or a weapon later in the discussions.

Put the well-being of your dog first

Agree to keep the focus on the well-being of your dog. It may sound simple and obvious, to do what is best for your dog, but it is an easy perspective to lose. Especially if things become heated, two people with the best of intentions can find their dialogue shift to a fight between them instead of focusing on the dog. Think about your dog's history, personality and what living situation would be ideal for them. Don't confuse what you want with what your dog wants or project your feelings onto your dog. Please refer to the next chapter if you are uncertain how to judge what might be best for the dog.

Consider shared custody wisely

Not all dogs cope well with moving permanently between two homes. For dogs who easily become anxious or stressed, it is certainly not fair. Living peacefully with a shared custody routine is much more likely for dogs who are easy-going, confident, healthy and have a mellow character. If your dog is elderly, a guarding or herding breed, prone to anxious behavior, comes from a traumatic background or doesn't handle change well, living between two homes is likely to be distressing for them. In addition, if you or your ex are not able to maintain a sense of peace between you then there is a good chance long term shared custody will be stressful for your dog. Detailed information on the pros and cons of shared custody appears in Chapter 7.

Agree to a three-to-six-month shared custody trial period

Only time will tell if your dog is happy with shared custody. Out of fairness to their dog, I always recommend my clients agree to a trial period of a few months to see how the dog copes. You will need to honestly assess your dog for signs of stress or changes in behaviour during a trial period of shared custody.

Sometime between the third or sixth month, you should be able to fairly assess whether your dog is happy with whatever new arrangement you have agreed to. Initially, many dogs seem fine moving between houses. Typically, clues that your dog is not adjusting to such a routine begin to show after a few weeks or months. Changes in personality, becoming reluctant to get into the car, anxious behavior, and having trouble adjusting during each transition normally start subtly and then become more pronounced with time. If this is the case for your dog, out of love and fairness to them, I strongly recommend the agreement change so that the dog has one primary home.

Another factor is that during this time, after divorce, your own circumstances or your ex's may change. Perhaps one of you will decide to move or get a job with a different schedule. These shifts in lifestyle might mean that shared custody is no longer realistic, or one of you may have a change of heart in such a way that you feel it is right to allow your dog to stay with the other person. Much can happen in a few months, and allowing a trial period gives the space for those changes to happen.

Be cautious about agreeing to let your ex visit the dog "anytime"

If your ex has agreed to let you keep the dog, it is a kind and reasonable thing to offer them visits whenever they want, especially if you are relieved that they are not fighting for custody of the dog. However, this means you are also giving your ex the permission to step in and out of your life for potentially many years to come. If you do not have any children that would otherwise keep you in contact, allowing for ongoing "anytime" visits like this will keep the two of you in contact and communication when you might be better off with a clear and clean separation from each other.

From the dog's side, visits from a previous pet parent can be unsettling. The reunion is certainly very exciting, yes, but the disappointment when that person drops off the dog and disappears is the hard part. If a dog is then left wondering when that special person will reappear at the door it can result in anxious and stressed-out behavior. Think of it this way, dogs adjust to living without the special person in their life, but when that person comes back into their life only to leave again and again, the dog has to deal with the sense of loss repeatedly.

I regularly work with clients who have to say goodbye to their dogs in situations that have nothing to do with divorce. For example, dogs who are fighting in the same household and one of them needs a new home, if people lose their job and cannot afford to keep their dog, if a dog is not able to adjust to a new baby, when the owner becomes chronically ill and is unable to care for their dog, when someone has adopted a dog that was just unsuitable for them due to the amount of energy or behavior challenges that dog may have. These clients who have to give their dog to a new home will often ask if they can visit the dog once he is settled in with his new family. I explain to them that it is not fair on the dog to pop in for visits only to leave again. This stops the dog from settling happily into their new home, they might start waiting at the door for a visit or wonder why "their people" came back for a visit but didn't take the dog with them. Whereas, if there are no visits, the transition is much easier, and dogs will form a bond with their new family much sooner.

As hard as it is to accept in the context of a divorce, the same dog behavior truths apply. Dogs will settle into a life with one of their guardians sooner without visits from someone they used to live with.

Focus on the future in negotiations

If a dog has lived with a couple for many years, the relationship has obviously been a long one; fights over the dog are then often more about what the dog stands for than the dog himself. To keep the negotiations productive, keep conversations about the future, *not* the past.

Although you should acknowledge who has taken the most interest in the dog historically, you need to look forward practically. Focus less on who paid for the animal, wanted him in the first place, or first owned him and more on who he is bonded with now.

The most relevant conversation about the dog is not about what life looked like in the past but what it will look like in the future. What will happen going forward? Often a person's living arrangements change after divorce. They may have to move to another residence or town, change jobs, or move in with someone else. Whose house is more suited to the animal?

Given the needs of your specific dog, who will be the most suitable to look after him? If you have a busy, active dog, who has the time and energy to meet all his exercise needs? If your dog is old, who can take better care of his medical needs and provide a quiet home? Who will be better equipped to deal with him when he grows old?

Summary questions

Can you separate your needs from the needs of your dog?

Are you willing to accept shared custody might be stressful for you dog?

Can you keep an open mind, even if it means giving up the dog?

Chapter 4
What You Need to Know
About Your Dog

During a mediation session, I have found it is not helpful or necessary to have the dog physically present. It can make it difficult during an hour or two discussion for the people involved to share their ideas if having the dog there is a distraction, not to mention that the dog is likely to find the situation highly stressful as well. In fact, having dogs sit in on mediation tends to be hugely stressful for them, I always imagine the dog thinks he is at the vet or some other scary place! What is necessary is a clear picture of the character, behavioral history, temperament, energy levels and breed of the dog, to make a clear-headed decision about what will be the best plan for the future of the dog. The history may be incomplete, or it may not all be in black-and-white, but it will give both you and me as the mediator a sense of what kind of life the dog has lived so far.

Whether you use a mediator or not, asking yourself the following questions will give you fresh insight into your dog. They will highlight how your dog handles change and stress and what their medical and exercise needs are. They are designed to help you separate what you want from what is best for the dog.

How old is your dog?
- A rescue dog may only have an approximate age.
- Dealing with a 10 to 12-year-old dog is very different from dealing with a one-year-old.
- Shared custody is best avoided in both young and old dogs. Pups rarely bond well with two different owners, while elderly dogs can find moving between homes unsettling.

What breed is your dog?

- What is the dog bred for? How does the breed type determine what he does, how he behaves and what he needs from you? How much exercise does your dog's breed typically need?

- If the dog is a purebred, genetics will usually play a more predictable role in determining his behavior than it would in a mixed breed. A rescue or a dog that isn't purebred may have characteristics of more than one breed.

In the following chapter, we look at how breed type can impact custody decisions given the wide variation of behaviors and care requirements seen in pet dogs.

Are there medical issues?

- Is the dog on any medication?

- What about joint issues or any condition that makes stairs difficult?

- Is the dog very susceptible to heat? To cold?

- Is the dog healthy? Shared custody is difficult for a sickly or physically unwell dog.

Did you get the dog as a couple, or did he belong to one of you first?

- If so, to whom?

How old was your dog when he came into your life?

- Was the dog a puppy, an adult, or a senior when you brought him home?

How many homes has the dog lived in?

- If he is a rescue dog, you may not know where he lived before coming to you.

- If you have moved, how did the dog adjust to a new place?

- Was he stressed or did he embrace the adventure?

- How well does your dog cope with change?

- If you're considering moving to an apartment, has your dog ever lived in an apartment before?

Is your dog an only dog?
- Was he always your only dog?

- Has he lived happily or unhappily with other animals before?

What was the dog's routine before and during separation?
- Who exercised your dog, and how often?

- Was the routine predictable and repetitive or spontaneous and different every week?

- Is your dog comfortable being home alone during the day?

How does he act around other dogs and people?
- Does he have a particular dog with whom he plays with at the dog park or play dates outside of the home?

- How does he act with strangers, both human and dog?

- Perhaps your dog finds it scary to accompany you to a picnic or barbeque. Perhaps he hides away from visitors or, alternatively, he wants to be with them. Some breeds have a genetic predisposition to be wary of strangers. Other dogs learn that as a coping mechanism due to their life circumstances.

- How is he with children? There may be no children in the dog's life yet but if one of the divorcees gets together with someone who has children, and suddenly the dog must live with a two- and six-year-old, he may not be able to handle it.

What are the current costs associated with your dog?
- How much is spent each month on your dog's food, medical needs, and insurance?

- What about other expenses, like grooming, training or day-care costs?

Is your dog used for working or showing purposes?
- Does your dog participate in any dog sports like agility, search and rescue, obedience, trick training, flyball, dog dancing, canicross trail running, herding, rally or nosework competitions? Who in the household does these activities with the dog?

- Is your dog showed in conformation events and/or used for breeding purposes?

Can you describe what your dog's behavior looks like when he is stressed or unhappy?

- Each dog is different, what does your particular dog do?

- Does your dog get louder or quieter when stressed?

- Does he withdraw or act tense or fearful?

- Or, you may have one of those happy go lucky dogs who never seems stressed or unhappy, or if they do get worried about something they get over it quickly!

Have you ever had professional help with your dog?

- Did the dog attend puppy school?

- Has the dog been to training classes and, if so, how often?

- Have you ever needed more serious professional help with your dog and, if so, what for?

- Was it resolved? Did both you and your ex feel the same way about it?

Does your dog have a history of separation anxiety or isolation distress?

- Was your dog hyper attached to you or your ex predominantly at any point?

- Were you able to solve your dog's separation anxiety issue and teach your dog to be comfortable being alone or without a specific individual?

- Does your dog still have to be carefully managed when alone?

Summary questions

Do you have a clear picture of your dog's history?

Can you describe your dog to a stranger, without a lot of emotion? Like you are describing a character in a movie?

What does your dog need for their best life? Consistent exercise? A quiet household? Walks on leash away from other dogs? Frequent socializing off lead?

Chapter 5
Breed Factors Which Can Influence Who Should Keep the Dog

There are many factors that come into play when the couple gets to the point of deciding who should keep the dog. I believe that the choice should be based on what is best for the dog. Easy to say, and hard to do. The breed or type of dog is often a key to making a well-informed decision. The answer will likely be different if the dog is a Chihuahua versus a Greyhound. I suggest that the person who keeps the dog is the one who can provide the most enriched life. Before going into a discussion of breed types, let's explore the concept of enrichment in more detail.

Who can provide the dog the most enrichment?

One of the complicating factors when it comes to determining what is enriching for the life of the dog, and which person is best able to provide it, is that dogs are among the most varied species on the planet. Think about the differences between Afghan Hounds, German Shepherds and English Bulldogs, for example; all the same species and yet so different from one another. Because of the vastly different physical and behavioral characteristics of dogs, there isn't a one size fits all answer to who should keep the dog after a divorce. The person best suited to keep a Border Collie is not always the best the person to keep a Maltese.

Research into how to provide an animal an enriched life began in earnest about 20 years ago in studies of zoo animals. A lone caged elephant is not living an enriched life. While enrichment can be defined in different ways, in general it means that a captive animal should, to the extent possible, be able to engage in behaviors that are natural to what that animal would do in the wild.

There are now many studies into how pet dogs can live more enriched lives. Research into this subject took at a great stride forward with the recent publication of the book *Canine Enrichment for the Real World* by Allie Bender and Emily Strong. While recognizing that dogs are pets and that constrains what they can be allowed to do, the authors provide advice on how to let dogs engage in such natural/instinctive behaviors as foraging, scent work, and retrieving while providing dogs healthy food, opportunities for exercise, and mental stimulation.

How breed types can impact custody decisions

Different breeds require different things to make them content and happy. For some dogs, a walk around the block is enough daily activity. Others may need a dedicated "job" to do every day to be satisfied and settled. The same is true for questions around custody, specifically can your breed of dog do well with a shared custody in the long run. There is not room here to discuss every single breed, but most dogs fall into one of ten breed types discussed below that share many common characteristics. (If you want more information, a great book to read is *Meet Your Dog* by Kim Brophey.) The information below about breeds is tricky because there always exceptions to common breed characteristics. This information is by no means set in stone and your dog could well be an exception to the norm, but nonetheless this is a good starting point! If you have a cross or mixed breed dog you will probably recognize characteristics from your dog's genetic background in the breed descriptions below.

Working dogs

Working dogs are a diverse set of breeds bred to do specific jobs. These jobs include guarding and protecting territory, as well as their human families, scent work and search and rescue. Examples are the Belgian Malinois, German Shepherds, Rottweilers, Dutch Shepherds and Dobermans. These breeds are very popular nowadays. And while they can be taught to stay on command, they can't be taught to be as mellow and easy going as a typical Golden Retriever. They are very territorial and will often not act well toward strangers. Owning one of these dogs is a serious commitment due to the amount of energy they have, and the time required to train them. If they don't get enough exercise and stimulation, they can become frustrated which can lead to aggressive, destructive or dangerous behaviors. Working dogs are not good candidates for shared custody because they will instinctually bond with their primary handler. Shared custody is rarely fair to these breeds as they have a strong sense of territory, whom they should listen to and whom they should protect. Moving back and forth from that primary person can cause stress and confusion. While they bond with the whole family, they form a primary attachment on whom they focus more than the others. Moving between families may be stressful for them.

Sled dogs

In some ways similar to the working dogs described above, Huskies, Malamutes and similar breeds were bred to pull sleds, and most will joyfully dig enormous holes in your yard if they don't get sufficient exercise. Even if they are adequately exercised, they may excavate the garden anyway because they love digging so much. But what they really need is to run. They need to move and get stuff done! They have big energy needs and require plenty of grooming due to their double-thick coat. Due to their high prey drive, if these dogs are not socialized with cats they are, sadly, prone to killing them. Because of their natural hunting instincts and desire to run, it is crucial these dogs have a husky-proof fence to keep them at home. Shared custody is a possibility with sledding dogs.

Herding dogs

This group includes Border Collies, Australian Shepherds, Australian Cattle Dogs, Shelties, and Welsh Corgis. They are intensely busy animals. In a perfect world they should live on farms (I say while having two of them in my own house) with livestock to look after! In order to meet the needs of herding dogs without an *actual herd* of animals, these dogs need to have their minds and bodies stimulated everyday with training games, intense activity and dedicated owners who are committed to giving them enough to think about every day. If not, these dogs will often compromise by trying to direct the movement of children on bicycles or cars driving by (especially those going in the opposite direction to the car they're in). The most important factor when it comes to custody is that a herding dog goes to the person who will exercise them the most. Like the working breeds mentioned above, shared custody is hard on these dogs because they naturally bond with one primary person.

Flock Guardian Dogs (FGD)

These include Great Pyrenees, Kuvasz, Anatolian Shepherds, Akbash and Maremma. FGDs are different from herding dogs in that they don't herd sheep and cattle but rather protect them from predators. In my experience, these dogs rarely make ideal family pets because they were bred to live outside with sheep and goats and guard them from wolves. FGDs are bred to work totally independent from the influence of a human being—unlike a Border Collie who naturally will take cues from a person. Their instincts tell them to scare away strangers and attack them if necessary. They need territory to defend and will demarcate one if there is no fence or wall to demarcate it for them. In South Africa, FGDs perform a great service protecting sheep from cheetahs and leopards. The big cats won't come close to the flock because the FGD is so effective at scaring them away. This means the farmers do not feel the need to hunt the cats to keep their livelihood safe. In the right context, these dogs are fantastic at doing what their instincts tell them to. On the other hand, in the wrong context, FGDs can become frustrated and dangerous. I've had more than one behavioral client where the FGD decided a woman was his "flock" and her husband the "wolf," and so the dog spent his time preventing the husband from coming anywhere near the wife! These dogs need something to protect and will find something—even if it doesn't need protecting. Shared custody is not a good idea for FGD because they're bred to be more bonded to their home than the human in it, so they have a very hard time transitioning if they must move to a different house. Moving between two living spaces can be highly stressful for these breeds and can lead to aggressive behavior.

Hunting dogs, gun dogs and bird dogs

Sometimes called "sporting dogs," these include Golden Retrievers, Labradors, Cocker Spaniels, German Shorthaired Pointers, Springer Spaniels and Irish Setters. These dogs were bred to aid hunters by pointing toward or retrieving fallen birds. Most of the time they are happiest while out in the field hunting. They are not naturally great guard dogs as they are easy-going, having been bred to tolerate gunshots, cold water and rough terrain. Goldens and Labs usually make good family dogs as they are typically tolerant of children, love to play fetch, and are easy to train. One of the reasons Labradors were first chosen to be guide dogs for blind people was because they simply aren't bothered by much and keep their cool under noisy or unsettling circumstances. Hunting dogs are generally good candidates for shared custody.

Hounds

This group can be divided in two. The first includes Beagles, Basset Hounds, Coonhounds, and Bloodhounds who were bred to work with people to hunt or track game with their noses. The second include Greyhounds, Whippets, and Borzoi who use their eyes (Sighthounds) to independently hunt game. Bred to follow their nose or eyes when hunting, hounds often are more difficult to control than other breeds once they see or smell something they want to pursue. They can be a challenge to train and may run away off-leash for adventures if they have not learned to come when called. Hound dogs are not overly territorial and not as prone to bond tightly with a single person so shared custody is a possibility if the hound dog was provided a steady upbringing and thus can handle change well. Sighthounds, however, tend to be much more sensitive to change than scent hounds so careful and honest evaluation of their individual temperament is important before considering a joint custody schedule.

Power/Bull Breed Dogs

Pitbull Terriers, Cana Corso, Akitas, American Bulldogs, Dogo Argentinos, Bull Terriers and Boerbulls are all examples of power breeds. They origins of these breeds vary, but they were all bred for either hunting or guarding purposes. What they all have in common is that they are incredibly strong, powerful animals. Well socialized power breeds can make excellent family dogs. However, the genetic inheritance, early exposure as puppies, lack of training or consistency can make them potentially very dangerous. The biggest challenge I see with power breeds are owners who are well meaning, but inexperienced or naïve about the potential for danger with such a powerful dog. This is due to no fault of the dogs themselves, but it is important to work with types of dogs with eyes wide open and be fully informed about the behavior history with each individual dog. When making decisions about custody for these breeds I recommend getting the guidance of a qualified dog professional with experience with these breeds to help determine what the best home situation is for these dogs, especially when there are other pets and children on the scene. See Chapter 12 for resources to find a dog professional

Terriers

Terrier dogs are small hunters, bred mostly in the United Kingdom to hunt mice and vermin during the Victorian era. Jack Russell Terriers, Fox Terriers, Lakeland Terriers, West Highland White Terriers,

Scotties and Airedales were bred to kill their prey and they are good at it. Some are avid diggers like Jack Russells, and in Germany, the Dachshunds. They're also noisy and bark because they were bred to tell their owner when they sensed a rat. "Hey, I've got a rat! I'm going to kill it! Yay!" Practically what this means is that if anything exciting happens, they'll bark because their genes tell them to. If anyone is researching dog breeds and reads that a particular breed makes an excellent watchdog, what that means is that the dog is very loud and barks a lot and Terriers fit the bill. As they do not necessarily tightly bond with one individual or living space, shared custody is possible. Terriers are typically hardy little dogs and can be very long lived.

Short-nosed dogs

This is quite a varied group of dogs who are very popular pets these days. French Bulldogs, Pugs, Old English Bulldogs, Boston Terriers, and Pekingese are examples. They tend to be low-energy dogs with short bursts of activity and may have chronic health troubles. Due to their breathing/panting issues they need to live in cool houses and preferably ones without stairs as their joints often cannot cope well with continuous climbing and descending. Shared custody with short-nosed dogs such as Pugs and Bulldogs is not always a good idea as these dogs can be very sensitive to stress and can be prone to physical reactions. Most important for these breeds is that the environment they live in is suitable and that the people caring for them have the knowledge, time and resources to care for them to keep them as healthy as possible.

Toy dogs

This group includes little dogs like Chihuahuas, Yorkies, Shih Tzus, Maltese, Toy Poodles and Miniature Dachshunds. There are many different personality types, and each dog must be carefully looked at on its own merit. They tend to be barkers, lap dogs, and some are very long lived. Shared custody can be overwhelming for any small dog; they are simply not as robust as bigger dogs. They are more physically impacted by stress than their larger counterparts.

How and who can provide the dog an enriched life?

Based on what was presented above and your own experience with the dog, hopefully both parties can decide who is better able to provide the best enrichment opportunities for the dog.

A change in custody can be hard for any dog. Knowing the characteristics of your dog's breed will help you to make an informed custody decision; couple this with your personal knowledge of your particular dog, his personality, history, health and age.

The age of the dog will affect their ability to adjust to new living arrangements, as older dogs will be less adaptable. The definition of old varies from breed to breed, and to the size and individual health of the dog. Great Danes may seem old when they're seven, for example, while Jack Russell Terriers are old when they're fifteen.

In the next chapter, we discuss shelter and rescue dogs. This category is so diverse, often including mixed breeds, that each dog must be assessed individually to decide who should get custody of the dog and whether shared custody would suit them or not.

Summary questions

What are the core characteristics of your dog's breed?

Does the genetic make up of your dog lend itself toward sole or shared custody?

Are you or your ex most able to meet the specific needs of your dog?

Chapter 6
Shelter and Rescue Dogs

When faced with a custody decision involving a shelter or rescue dog, one of the first things you need to establish is if the dog easily handles stressful situations or gets overwhelmed and fearful when life circumstances change. Once you can answer this question clearly, then you can more honestly picture if your dog is better suited to live with one of you and/or will adapt to shared custody, visitations or an unusual schedule.

Shelter and rescue dogs come in every shape, temperament, age, breed and background you can imagine. Perhaps your rescue dog lived in a shelter for some months before being adopted or, even more extreme, your rescue might have been near death starving or sick and needed tremendous time and care to recover. On the other hand, you may have taken a perfectly healthy, happy dog into your home because his previous owner was unable to care for him.

In my experience as a Certified Dog Behaviour Consultant, I have found when it comes to shelter or rescue dogs, they are often the "best or the worst" when it come to their responses to stress or unusual things happening in their environment. Some recuse dogs who come from a hard life before getting adopted may go through life as peaceful souls who never seem to be phased by much. They will happily travel, meet new people and dogs and be sweet about it. Imagine a dog with the qualities of Buddha, peaceful regardless of their surroundings. On the other hand, many adopted dogs may not trust the world around them, regardless of how wonderful their new home is. Such dogs may react fearfully to new things or have any of a host of anxiety responses to being alone or in social situations.

Some of them can absolutely be helped with appropriate behavior modification, but they will generally have to be managed carefully and for the rest of their lives.

Individual history and behavior

The responses of shelter and rescue dogs to changes in life circumstances will vary hugely depending on their personal history, genetic make-up and individual character. It is impossible for me make any sort of generalization about these dogs in the context of divorce and custody because each dog comes from a different background, both genetically and in terms of life experiences, good or bad. Instead, you should start to seek answers with four questions about the dog to establish a clear picture of their history and character:

- How old was your dog when it entered the shelter?
- Was there abuse or neglect in their background?
- How adaptable was your dog to new people, places or routines?
- Are there any challenging behaviors you will likely have to manage, like anxiety when being alone, fearful or aggressive reactions to any people or other dogs?

Be aware that the amount of information a shelter or rescue organization can provide you about the dog's history may vary widely. A well-funded shelter may have the time and resources to gather information, others may not.

If your dog was adopted as a puppy

If the dog was adopted or rescued as a puppy and was provided a good environment and was socialized, it is likely that he will become an adaptable adult. When I work with my clients who have a shelter/rescue dog who was adopted at four months, it is very different than working with a dog rescued at four years old. Adopted pups often are more likely to become well-adjusted adults.

Interestingly, when pups are around five or six months old (depending on the size of the puppy) they grow into a new phase of their development and go through what is called a "fear and/or sensitive period." As they transition out of the adorable, naive, puppy breath phase, where the world is a wonderful, curious place, they begin to remember things they experience that are dangerous or scary. If something potentially spooky happens to a puppy at four months old, it won't necessarily affect him or create much of a memory. But one of the fascinating things about dogs is that if the exact same thing happens at about six months, the fear can stay with them forever. For example, if you accidentally drop a pot in the kitchen and it makes a loud noise, your six-month-old pup may start being reluctant to go into the kitchen when you are cooking. Or if they experience booming thunder for the first time or a child pulls his ear until it hurts, those experiences are much more likely to have a lasting impact than they would on a young puppy. These scary experiences can be ameliorated with good guidance and techniques. See Chapter 12 for information on finding qualified help.

This means if you obtained a rescue dog before six months, it is more likely that your dog is okay unless he was severely abused. Even if he grew up in less than an ideal setting, the dog will be more able to grow into a happy and trusting adult.

Shelter/rescue dogs with a history of abuse or neglect

Dogs who have experienced abuse in their lives are most likely to struggle with the changes in their households that can happen during a divorce. Regardless of breed, dogs who have been previously ill-treated are very likely to be very sensitive to current conflict around them, such as the emotional outbursts, which can happen during divorce.

Any dog who has been neglected or abused will likely employ the sort of same strategy they did to protect themselves in the past. In a household suddenly full of conflict, a dog who was easy going may start growling at people or they might spend their time hiding in the far corner of your house, trying to be as unnoticeable as possible. If your dog is showing signs of intense fear or displaying aggression towards people, seek out qualified professional help for guidance. Whatever your dog's reaction to your own emotional state might be, don't take his behaviors personally, your dog is trying to cope in the only way he knows how.

If you and your ex are fighting, it can be pure hell for a traumatized shelter or rescue dog. Your dog shouldn't witness your fights or have to double as a tissue because one of you is crying into his neck at a difficult handoff. If you feel like you cannot cope without being around your dog during this difficult time, you are likely relying on your dog too much to be your emotional support. No dog should be asked to hold the weight of this emotional burden for you, but especially shelter dogs. If you and your ex are highly emotional, it may be the kindest thing to your dog to find a trusted third party to keep your dog until the situation is resolved. Having someone else care for the dog for a limited time is usually much better than the two of you trading the dog back and forth if it is stressful for him.

How adoptable was your shelter/rescue dog?

Hopefully you got your dog from a progressive organization which takes the time to evaluate the adoptability of each dog they take in. Many shelters conduct what are termed "temperament tests" on the dogs that come into their care, the results of which may help you decide how well the dog deals with stress and change and therefore make a better custody decision.

These tests vary but most show how the dog handles meeting strangers, reactions to sudden sounds, and being touched or handled. The results of these tests can predict how the dog will react to visitors, sounds, and new places. If your dog is unphased by things changing around them and responds to new circumstances with curiosity, then you probably have a naturally adaptable pooch. If on the other hand, you have a dog who needs to be carefully introduced to new people, unfamiliar situations or manged carefully around specific types of animals or people, it is safe to say your dog is not particularly adaptable. There are several books you can refer to to do your own temperament tests to help you decide how adaptable your dog is. Author and shelter expert Sue Sternberg is considered the expert on temperament testing. Her book *Assessing Aggression Thresholds in Dogs* is a great reference.

Is shared custody right for my shelter dog?

Dogs who prove to be adaptable enough to handle shared custody the best are easy-going with a mellow character. If you have a dog like this who is a well-adjusted and contented soul, then shared custody is something you and your ex can think about.

If your dog falls into the category of being wary of the unexpected, whether people, places, or other animals, then I do not recommend having your dog move between you and your ex. For these dogs, it is kinder for them if they live in one home with a predictable routine. Moving between homes, even if you both love the dog, will likely prove to be unsettling for them and make their anxiety or other behavior issues worse over time. In this situation, your dog should live with the person who has the time, and ability, to best manage and work with them.

Summary questions

Does your dog enjoy new people, experiences and unfamiliar places?

What is your dog's reaction to intense emotions, like shouting at sports on tv, being around people who have been drinking alcohol or when they are crying?

Do you think there is abuse or mistreatment in your dog's background?

Chapter 7
Shared Custody
Pros and Cons

It is becoming almost an automatic assumption that when people split up, they must share custody of their pets. Sharing the dog may seem like the best way to avoid the heartbreak of saying goodbye or because people feel that they made a lifetime commitment to the dog that they cannot go back on. But shared custody should not be such a common course of action, in my opinion, as it is often very hard on dogs. Shared custody can be unsettling and stressful for them.

Don't tell yourself that you are doing shared custody for the dog. Shared custody is something you do for yourselves. The dog does not struggle as hard as you do to say goodbye. Shared custody is something that a dog *tolerates*, if it can. You need to ask yourself, "Can our dog handle shared custody? Is it fair for me to expect this of my dog?"

If you don't have human children, just the dog or dogs, and you want shared custody, it means that you will continue to have contact with your ex for what could be a long time. Are you and your ex prepared to prolong your relationship in this way? Do you want your ex to know what you're up to? Will you and your ex try to micromanage each other when the dog is not with you? Opting for shared custody sometimes creates a situation in which someone can stay connected or involved in an ex's life, keeping tabs on them, when it would be healthier to move on. It may not be intentional, but can be driven by some subconscious refusal to let go.

If you keep the dog and the separation is amicable, you might generously invite your ex to visit the pet; if they keep the dog, they too might say that you are welcome to visit. But this may not be the wisest idea for anyone; saying goodbye to the ex and the dog may be better in the long run. Even though you are no longer in a relationship, the dog becomes a connection between you and your ex that can be very challenging to sustain.

Will shared custody suit your dog?

There are certainly dogs who handle a shared custody schedule just fine. Here are some guidelines.

Shared custody works best when:

- The dog is easy going, not prone to anxiety or reactivity.
- The dog enjoys new things, places and people.
- The dog's guardians can hand them over peacefully without emotional hellos and goodbyes.
- The dog is young and confident.
- The dog is bonded with children and will move when they do (children can become the steady factor for dogs moving between guardians).

Shared custody is not advisable when:

- The dog is older, less adaptable, frail or sick.
- The people involved are antagonistic.
- Handovers become an endlessly stressful series of separations and reunions.
- The dog is a rescue with a history of abuse or many different homes.
- The dog has clearly formed a strong bond with one person.
- The dog is a guarding, livestock, or herding breed and become attached to their home territory as much as to the people in them.

Trial periods, dog walkers, schedules and other tips

In Chapter 3, I advised that those opting for shared custody agree to a three-to-six-month trial period after which they honestly reassess the situation. During this time, it will become clear if shared custody is working well or not for you, your ex and your dog. Human emotions sometimes settle down after a few months and one of the two people might realize that they are comfortable letting the ex keep the dog and they are able to say goodbye. Meanwhile, after a few months, any early signs of stress caused by shared custody will have surfaced in the dog, indicating whether they are coping with the changes. If not, adjustments can be made, people can revisit their decisions and the reasons for them; if no one is willing to budge, an expert can be called in to evaluate the dog's condition and work with the guardians toward a less stressful solution for the dog.

There are different options in terms of sharing custody schedules. A lot depends on people's work schedules and how close they live to one another. I've had situations where one ex works all week and the other doesn't, so the former takes the dogs for weekends purely because it works out schedule-wise, and for them it has proven to be successful. Generally, longer visits are better as then the transitions back and forth are minimized. The goodbyes and hellos are the most stressful part of shared custody. Weeks are better than days; two-week visits often work well or even a month on and a month off schedule, especially as exes will have to see one another at every handoff, unless you have a neutral third party involved.

Another tip, if you do not want to interact with your ex, is to use a third party to help facilitate the exchanges. For some dogs this is best done with a dog walker/dog taxi who picks the dog up at one house and either walks or drives the dog to the other house. This can minimize the tension and emotions during the hand off moment. Some of my clients choose to do something similar at a doggy daycare: one person drops off the dog on a certain day and the other picks the dog up.

If there are children, it may work well for the dog to move between parents with them, which is helpful because it offers more structure and predictability to the transition. We will look more closely at dogs and children in Chapter 10. The dog may be less bonded to the children than you think and prefer to stay with one of the adults. If a dog's strongest bond is with one of the parents, it is better for that parent to have sole custody and for the children to see the dog when they stay with that parent.

What is often hardest for the dog are random visits from you or your ex. Let's say there's no shared custody, but something pulls at the ex's heart strings and they really want to see the dog suddenly. This can be stressful for a dog who, at this stage, is settled. They're used to living with one guardian, and all is well. After the excitement of a visit from their former person, then they leave again. Those exhilarating visits followed by the void of the person being gone can lead some dogs to sit at the door, wondering if every approaching car or every footstep belongs to the guardian who went away. *Maybe they're coming back,* the dog thinks. *Or maybe not.* You end up with stressed-out behaviors, especially if the missing person just shows up at the door, demanding to see the dog. This is the most unsettling thing for the animal. There are other ways to check whether the dog is okay. If you're not the one to keep the dog, the kindest thing you can do is say goodbye and leave them to their new life. It's like taking off a Band-Aid; the quicker it's off, the better.

Shared custody and stress

I will say this more than once in this book, moving between two homes can be hard on dogs in the long run and its one of the reasons I often do not recommend it. Here is real life story, involving clients of mine, that shows why:

A gentleman called me for help because his two adult Dachshunds, sweet little sausage or wiener dogs, were peeing on his couch. "Okay," I assured him, "That's something I work with all the time." I went to his house to meet him and the dogs, to determine the root cause of the misplaced peeing so I could create a behavior modification plan to address it. After assessing the history of the behavior, I learned that they had not been couch-wetters to begin with. It had been going on for around eight months, but it only happened every two weeks and lasted for about three days. "That's quite interesting," I remarked, "What happens every two weeks?"

"Well, every other weekend they go to my ex's house," he said. "When they come home to my house they pee inside for a few days." "Aah! That's a pretty clear indication that it's not a happy arrangement for them," I realized. One of the ways dogs try to relieve stress is to repeatedly pee in an area.

When I teach training classes, one of the ways I identify confident dogs from nervous ones is because the latter pee all over the place while the former will pee only once or twice in a public place. The nervous dogs are saying, "I was here, and I was here, and I was here…and I was also here! Everybody must know this!" It's a myth dogs pee everywhere to try and be the boss; a better way to describe it is that adult dogs will pee repeatedly to try to establish themselves in a new space when they feel *out of place* and the peeing stops when they feel more at ease there. Whereas dogs who feel at home in a property or in a public space will not normally feel the need to spread their scent on any available tree or couch!

I said to the gentleman with the Dachshunds, "The dogs are showing you in the only way they can that this transition is not working for them. How do you feel about the arrangement?"

"I'm not happy about it, no," he confided, "Every time I drop the dogs off, there's a fight. Every time I pick them up, there's a fight." Sometimes his ex's new boyfriend was there, and it was an uncomfortable situation. It was uncomfortable for the dogs, too—dramatic, overly emotional. It wasn't a clean handover. It was impossible for the dogs to contextualize the divorce and emotional fallout as humans can.

"Let me know if your ex will speak to me," I suggested. The peeing inside behavior only started when the shared custody routine did, meaning the two situations were linked to each other. I had an honest conversation with the ex-partner of my client. I explained to her that the dogs were not doing well with their current schedule and the peeing inside was their way of showing that. She did agree that having the dog's every second weekend was not fair to continue if the dogs were unhappy. To test my theory, the dogs stayed at the gentlemen's place for two months and the peeing behaviour stopped. Both the people and the dogs breathed a sigh of relief; the ex was able to close the door on their continuing communication and the dogs settled into a happy life in one home.

How to deal with the dog's stress

Divorce is stressful; there is no real way around that. Now that you have custody of the dog (or shared custody), you may end up with a worried dog along with all the other pressure that you are under. Learning what you need to know to deal with stress is a key factor in providing an enriched life for your dog. And on top of everything you are dealing with, the guilt of thinking your dog is suffering can make everything worse. It can help to understand that the stress a dog might feel during your divorce is not necessarily any worse than it might have felt during other times of upheaval in your life. If you had lost a job, or a loved one had passed away, your dog would also have been affected by undercurrents of tension and sadness. It is not possible to provide a problem-free environment for your dog because your life is eventful and will entail both minor and momentous changes that affect your mood and behavior and, subsequently, that of the dog. There is no way you can protect your dog from the inevitable ups and downs of life by trying to hide your emotions, pretending everything is okay. Your dog is too perceptive for that. But you can learn to recognize and hopefully alleviate stress in your dog.

As with humans, dogs experience stress that is beneficial (eustress) and stress that is harmful (distress). Eustress occurs when there are challenges with which one can cope, bringing happiness, excitement and vigor; but distress is caused by oppressive issues leading to a meltdown. Good and bad stress may manifest in similar ways, but one is related to a happy demeanor while the other is related to gloom.

You can think of stress as showing up in two ways, situational and long-term. Situational stress is a reaction on the part of the dog to events that make them uncomfortable such as going to the vet's office, thunderstorms, having his nails clipped, or even a person moving close to a dog and staring right at him. While dogs may bounce back from such events, there are ways to help them deal with situational stress. You will see in the next section that you can learn to read signals your dog uses to let you know of their discomfort.

Long-term stress can be harder to spot. This is due to gradual changes in a dog's life. Getting less exercise, people changing their attitude toward a dog, health issues, not being able to rest sufficiently during the day because the dog goes to a busy doggy day-care full time, a home continually in a tense state, suddenly spending hours alone every day, living with new animals, children or babies in the house These all have the potential to overwhelm a dog for different reasons.

Body language as a way of communicating stress

Dogs are experts as reading your body language as well as the body language of other dogs. What is missing in many cases is the ability of a person to read the body language of his or her dog. Dogs display a wide variety of stress signals via body language that you can learn to read!

We need to be smart and recognize stress when it shows up in their behavior and body language. So how can you tell how stressed your dog is and what can you do?

Stress signs to watch for

One of the clearest signs of stress in dogs of all types is when there is a change in their behavior or they act out of character. It's not to send an intentional message to their owners but because a dog's behavior reflects their internal state. I'm a big fan of telling people that dogs are always honest; their body language and their behavior clearly show us how they are doing. The expression of their stress depends on the dog's breed, character, age, etc. The same is true for people; some of us get very quiet and withdrawn when we are not doing well, and others may get louder and angrier. A dog that was previously sedate starts overreacting to stimuli, becoming excited about everything. He may have enjoyed the neighbor's children but now becomes annoyed by them. He may never have been the kind of dog that chews a chair leg or burrows under a fence and runs away but starts doing this after going through a change.

Dogs often utilize what Turid Rugaas in her book *On Talking Terms with Dogs* has labeled "displacement behaviors." These behaviors are used to communicate a dog's unease with a situation, not only with other dogs but with people as well. It is a signal that the dog is uncomfortable with a situation. If you know what to look for, you may be able to avoid the dog reacting aggressively or shutting down. You may see a dog utilize displacement behaviors at a pick-up or hand-off, especially if they are fearful of transitioning from one house to another for example. While there are many such displacement behaviors, here are six common ones you may encounter.

1. Tail-tucking

What happens to your dog's tail when they say hello or goodbye to you or your ex? Tucking a tail down for a dog who does not normally do that during a greeting can be a sign the dog is uneasy. Dogs drop their tails toward the ground or curl them toward their belly, hiding their scent to stay inconspicuous.

2. Yawning

Yawning is a very common displacement behavior used to dissipate tension. In fact, some people do this as well! If a dog is not tired but is uneasy, this is a signal of unease with the situation.

3. Avoiding eye contact

Turning the head away from people is another frequently seen displacement behavior showing that the dog is uncomfortable, for example when a stranger comes too close.

4. Nose licking

While dogs stick their tongues out or lick their noses as a way of showing other dogs that they are friendly, they also flick their tongues across their noses as a signal to say, "I'm worried and not a threat. Please don't hurt me."

5. Shaking off

Dogs naturally shake their whole bodies after getting wet, to dry themselves, or after a nap, to wake themselves up. But if a dry dog has been awake a long time and shakes off like they are wet, they are signaling unease. It means they are tense and worried.

6. Excessive panting

When dogs start panting when they are not hot, they may be stressed and utilize this as a signal their discomfort.

Problem behaviors relating to long-term stress

If your dog displays the following behaviors, first rule out physical problems or sickness by having him checked by a veterinarian. *If there is no medical reason* for the behavior change, he may be suffering from long-term stress caused by untenable circumstances. I do not recommend simply relying on anxiety-reducing medication to reduce stress in dogs. While medication can be a helpful tool, it is much kinder and healthier to understand and remedy the reason for their unease and address the root cause of the situation. To learn more about all types of stress in dogs I recommend you read *The Stress Factor in Dogs* by Kristina Spaulding.

1. Aggressive behavior

Mild to serious aggressive behavior toward people or dogs is a common sign of tension or stress. One of the most troubling signs can be a short temper in a dog that was not aggressive before; they might suddenly have a short fuse and growl or snap at people, who might find it hard to understand why. Because they are stressed, proximity becomes harder to bear and they have less patience with people or dogs who approach them.

2. Housetraining troubles

For dogs who are already reliably housetrained, if they suddenly start messing inside, it is likely a stress response. Dogs who feel out of place in a home may pee inside in an attempt to relive anxiety and reestablish their scent inside. In layman's terms, I like to describe worried dogs who start peeing inside as feeling "lost" and are using their scent to feel like they belong there.

3. Destructive behavior

If a dog demolishes things regularly, the first question to ask is whether they are getting enough daily exercise. Busy dogs may be bored left on their own all day and find it distracting to rip stuff up. If they are well-exercised, however, and still obsessed with obliterating parts of your house, they may be doing so to relieve tension.

4. Social shyness

Needing time alone is normal and healthy for dogs of all ages, but if avoiding people and dogs is out of character for your dog, or they become inclined to seek solitude instead of social interaction, it is worth paying attention.

5. Loss of appetite

As with all the other behaviors on this list, loss of appetite occasionally happens, but when it happens regularly or the dog loses weight, it could be because they are too full of worry to eat.

6. Skin problems, shedding and foot chewing

Dogs can start chewing the pads of their feet or licking small raw spots on their fur for no medical reason other than stress. It is a way of self-soothing. Sudden hair loss can also occur due to nervousness. Like all of the examples here, it is most important to have these conditions checked out by a veterinarian you trust (not the internet!) when they suddenly appear. However, do be honest with your vet about the upheaval in your home life so they are aware there may be lots of different factors to look at.

Training tips for alleviating stress

If you got the dog, or you and your ex are going to try shared custody, plan to assess the dog for signs of stress for at least the first three months. If symptoms of long-term stress (described above) are present, out of fairness to the dog, consider re-evaluating the kind of life you have arranged for him. It's important to get a picture of your dog's character and routine before the divorce, so you can see whether, after the divorce, he still reacts to things the way he normally did.

For dogs who are stressed or seem uneasy in some way, first check on the most important things like their physical health, sense of peace at home, and routines around mealtimes. If those needs are all being met and your dog still appears to need something more, add some activities that use their legs, mouths, noses, and their minds.

1. Using their legs

Exercise can be a great stress reliver for dogs. Another way to think about this is if you have been too busy or overwhelmed to give your dog their normal amount of exercise, it will be harder for your dog to be settled and peaceful. Be mindful of course of the physical limitations of your dog, but more exercise is almost always a good thing! Dogs that are tired will rest better and cope more easily with whatever is going on in their life. That is the best, simplest, healthiest way to keep dogs sane and happy and sleeping well.

Try to get your dog moving for runs, walks or trips to dog-appropriate places where they can get tired—what I call *big pant tired*. Once a day your dog should move enough to need a full, open-mouth pant to cool down. This means your dog has extended their body well to their full speed or capacity, a heathy state for animals to get to!

A Pug and an Irish Setter will need a different amount of exercise to reach big pant tired. Using your dog's age, breed, and general health, make sure you are giving your dog an appropriate amount of activity for them as individuals. If you have dogs of very different sizes or ages you will need to give them different amounts of activity. A five-month-old pup and an adult dog of the same size should have separate exercise opportunities, so the pup is not over-worked, or the mature dog under-worked!

During difficult times, don't hesitate to get outside support in the form of a dog walker or doggy day-care if this is a suitable option for your dog. If your friend is going through a divorce and has a dog, offering to take the dog for walks would undoubtedly be appreciated.

2. Using their mouths

Chewing is a great natural stress reliever for dogs. Dogs need good things to chew on all the time but especially during times of tension or worry. I love enrichment toys that I can stuff food into to get dogs productively chewing. Your dog is going to eat anyway so make the most of it and use his normal meals to exercise his jaw too. There are so many stuffed food toy options out there!

There are many other good chewing items that your dog will enjoy. I don't mean toys for playing with like rope, balls, or stuffed toys but chewables that your dog will safely chew up and swallow. They must be so delicious they will want to chew it up right away. For example, you can buy dried duck feet, beef tracheas, beef or ostrich bones, salmon skins, Greenies, etc. As always, check with your vet that the chew you would like to give your dog is safe.

3. Using their noses

Here are two easy ideas to get your dog to use his nose.

First, scatter-feed your dog, provided you are feeding your dog dry food, not wet or raw food. Spread your dog's food in an area of about 3 feet by 3 feet, either on the grass in your garden or on a clean carpet in your home. This will give your dog a chance to sniff out each little pellet.

Secondly, the simplest way to get a dog to use his nose is on something we dog professionals call a decompression walk. This is a walk or a hike in an area where a dog is allowed to tune out from everything, go at his own pace and sniff anything he wants to. A decompression walk means you are not asking your dog to do anything specific like heel, fetch or play with a big group of dogs. If your dog is reliable off lead, then take them to a dog-safe outdoor area where they can move in front of you at their own pace and sniff and explore. A long leash of about 6 or 9 feet also works well. When your dog stops to sniff, stop with them. Allowing dogs the time to get lost in their nose settles them down beautifully.

My busy working dogs get a decompression walk every morning. I take them to a forest for an off-lead walk. I leave all my fun training toys at home. This is their time to *just be dogs*: run, pee, sniff around and say *hi* to the occasional dog pal who walks by. Later in the day we do training games, play fetch and practice agility or scent training. Scent training teaches dogs to detect scents and indicate that they've detected them; this is mentally and physically stimulating for them and helps increase their bond with their humans.

4. Using their minds

Car rides, training classes, walking in unfamiliar places or extra social time are some ways to stimulate your dog's intellect. Most dogs find this activity very enriching. My favorite way to keep a dog's mind busy is by teaching tricks. I first got into trick training out of necessity when I was faced with my own busy dogs and was desperately looking for ways to keep their minds stimulated and content. There are wonderful resources listed here at the end of the book available to you in the form of book or videos on how to teach your dog tricks.

Summary questions

When there are new relationships, job opportunities, or other life changes how will you feel about the impact shared custody with your dog may have on the next phase of your life?

If your dog does not handle shared custody well, can you both agree that one of you should have sole custody?

Can you be creative about helping your dog use their nose, mouth and mind to stay relaxed during times of transition or confusion?

Chapter 8
Keeping More
Than One Dog

Often households have more than one dog. What then? Can you separate a pair or group of dogs? Is it heartbreaking for the dogs to be split up? How do you know what is the right thing to do?

Most people assume that dogs shouldn't be separated. That dogs who have grown up together should always be in the same home, like human siblings. However, dogs don't just automatically love one another because they live together, even if they grew up with each other.

Claire and Jeff had two small cross breeds. The older dog, Billy, was about 13 years old and had arthritis in his elbows which meant he couldn't walk very far. Their younger dog, Lola, was a year-and-a-half and very playful. She loved to race around on the couches all day and constantly tried to get Billy to chase her. Billy romped for only a few minutes each morning and then spent most of his day trying to avoid Lola's roughhousing.

Early in the divorce process, Jeff and Claire asked me for help to decide what should happen with their dogs. Jeff wished to keep Billy and look after him in his twilight years and let Claire keep busy little Lola. Initially, Clare was adamant that the dogs should stay together and live with her. After we all discussed this, Claire saw that it would be kinder to Billy to let him live as an only dog during his retirement. His arthritis caused him pain and while he enjoyed the short, daily playtime with Lola, she made the rest of his life exhausting. Lola, in turn, was frustrated by her boring pack mate who basically ignored her as much as he could. Billy would tire easily and Lola was unable to play games with him. They were not well-matched because their energy needs were so different.

Thankfully, this story ended well for the dogs and the people. Jeff took custody of Billy who was able to sleep in a warm blanket for long periods of time. Claire found Lola a younger, more suitable dog sibling so that she had someone to play with whenever she wanted.

Should dogs be split up?

The vast difference in size, temperament and energy levels of dogs means that not all are well-matched as playmates or friends.

Relationships between dogs can be put into three broad categories:

1. **Bonded friends.** These dogs are the best of pals, have a strong bond and enjoy each other. Dogs that have a similar energy level, body robustness, maturity level and temperament are the most likely to be close friends and very attached to each other. A tough little Jack Russell Terrier may love wrestling with a huge Rottweiler pal, or two mature small breed dogs might enjoy napping together during the day, happily relaxed in each other's company.

2. **Roommates.** Some dogs live together peacefully and get along well, but they don't have a close bond. These sorts of dogs will peacefully share a home, but don't seek out much social interaction with each other; they basically ignore each other. This is common when dogs have very different ages, energy levels or breed type. A typical Husky and Lhasa Apso, for example, would have very different ideas of a good time.

3. **Barely tolerant or incompatible.** There are dogs who would be better not living together. There may be an underlying tension in this dog combination that is mild or serious. Perhaps there were previous fights between the dogs, or they seem to be walking on eggshells around each other all the time. Or dogs of very different ages, like in the example above with Lola and Billy, may not be as happy together as you think. If there is a younger, very energetic bouncy dog living with an elderly, dog it can overwhelm the older dog who, instead of being able to sleep happily much of the day, has no option but to be the unwilling plaything for a busy adolescent dog.

As a rule of thumb, if your dogs are closely bonded, it is better to keep them together if possible. For other dogs who are peaceful, but not besties, they really can adjust fine to living in a home without the other. And for the third category, a divorce can be a perfect excuse to allow the dogs to separate from each other and live in different homes.

It can be a great kindness to separate incompatible pairs of dogs. Whether it is due to age, size or individual dynamics, not all dogs love all other dogs.

Keep them together or not?

How do you know if the dogs are bonded friends or roommates and can be expected to remain that way? Here are a couple of indicators.

Regular social interaction. Do your dogs play together without a person involved? Do they chase each other, wrestle, explore the garden, tug with toys, or otherwise engage by themselves during the day? Or if they are more sedate souls, maybe they simply follow each other around most of the time, groom each other or otherwise stay very connected during their daily activities.

Dogs that regularly choose to sleep together on the same bed or near each other are probably also well-bonded. If there are four pets in the house and two of them like to rest together, or lie close together every night, they are likely a bonded pair. Of course, some dogs are so hairy they never want to sleep near anyone because they get too hot. Puppies tend not to be very selective about where they sleep, they will normally just find the coziest spot. But adult dogs will only sleep next to another dog or a person they trust. Generally, if a dog sleeps with a person, to smell the smell of the person while they sleep, it's a sign of the dog being bonded to them.

None of my own four dogs are particularity cuddly dudes, they never sleep close to each other but they all like to play with one another, so it's not all black-and-white. In order to honestly assess the bond between dogs you need to look at the whole picture of their lives together. Like people, even good dog pals may have the occasional small spat or short, harmless fight. If they fight often, or if it requires constant management from you to keep the house peaceful so they don't have an altercation, they would probably be happier apart.

Even dogs who are bonded can recover from being split up if the people involved have no choice. There are heartbreaking situations where there is simply no option but to separate dogs who clearly care for each other. But even in those tough circumstances, with time, dogs can bounce back more easily than we may think they do.

Factors influencing behavior toward one another

To figure out which of the three types of relationships your dogs have, look at the following four factors:

1. **Size of the dogs in relation to each other**
2. **Temperament/energy levels**
3. **Age difference**
4. **Engagement with each other**

First, let's consider two breeds that are ancient cousins with the same ancestry: a 100-pound Mastiff and a 10-pound Pug. They have a similar shape but the significant difference in size means that these breeds do not normally play together. It is potentially dangerous for the small dog, who could get hurt playing with such a heavy dog, and frustrating for the bigger dog who prefers a similarly proportioned dog to wrestle with. The bigger dog may grow bored, unable to really throw his full power and weight into playing, while the smaller dog may be perpetually nervous about getting harmed should the game get out of hand.

Thus, *size matters*. A newly married couple at my training school discovered this to be true. They couldn't agree on which dog to get and eventually decided that it would be cute to have a *his and hers*: a Bull Terrier and a Yorkie. They hoped that the dogs would live as happily ever after as they intended to do, but they would have had to be an extremely rare sort of Bull Terrier and an extremely rare sort of Yorkie to pull that off. The two breeds generally cannot play together because Bull Terriers are super strong and intense, while even the most magnificently confident Yorkie simply does not have the size to play safely with a Bully! This is not fault of either dog; expecting that a large dog will have to learn to very gently accommodate a tiny friend is not always realistic or fair.

When people ask for my advice on getting a friend for their current dog, I always tell them to get a dog of a similar size and weight so that they can play comfortably with each other. Let's say you have a short Scottish Terrier, a good pal for him would be something like a Westie, Schnauzer, Jack Russell Terrier, Dachshund or of course a cross breed of the same sort of dimensions. Bringing home a tall German Short-Haired Pointer puppy would be a nightmare for a Scotty because the puppy would already be taller than him! Imagine a parallel universe where people varied as much in size as dogs and you, at six feet tall, were asked to babysit a friend's toddler who was 15 feet tall! How would you manage such a thing?

Age also matters. Dogs do better with dogs of the same basic size and energy level, which is usually determined by age and breed. A pair of Labradors who are two years apart, for example, are a perfect combination of size and age and would be harder to separate than dogs of different dimensions and years. Dogs who are at the same phase of life are more likely to want to do the same doggy activities. A pair of sweet older dogs will both sleep at the same time, have a little bit of energy in the morning and evening and probably be content to rest together and contemplate the clouds together for the rest of the day. And younger dogs, or dogs still in the active mid part of their lives, will likely enjoy playing more games with each other. So it is easier to keep dogs together when they are of a similar age.

If you have dogs of very different ages, there is a good possibility that separating them will be okay for them, depending on what is the best plan for you and your ex.

It is a common misconception that getting a puppy will bring life back into an older dog. Often older dogs find puppies exhausting and irritating. Imagine sending a busy toddler to live full time with an elderly person who is at the phase of their life when playing cards with friends is their idea of a good time. A visit from a toddler would likely be wonderful, but to be around that sort of endless energy all day would actually be exhausting for them.

Younger dogs are more adaptable than older dogs when it comes to most things, including saying goodbye to a friend. If you have a pair of dogs, and they're eight and ten years old respectively and have lived together peacefully and happily all those years, I would not recommend splitting them up. Even for dog pairs who are good friends, if circumstances are such that separating them is necessary, the younger the dogs are, the sooner they will bounce back from such a transition.

A useful product for bonded dogs who have to be split up and are mourning due to the death of a dog friend or any other stressful period, is a pheromone collar that releases stress-reducing phero-mones that are activated by their body heat. These are wonderful tools and I frequently recommend them to my clients. There are also pheromone collars and wall plug ins specifically for cats. Helpful websites for more information are listed in the resources at the end of the book.

Practical advice for the separation moment

For pairs of dogs who will now live in different homes, it is less distressing for the dogs if the good-bye process happens as gently as possible. Do your best not to get emotional yourself and allow for some time of separation, especially if the dogs are bonded with each other and there is simply no choice but to have the dogs live in different homes. Some of my clients have tried to "get the dogs used to it" by having them spend a few days apart and then a few days together. This routine only prolongs the adjustment time for the dogs. It, of course, also extends what may be a final goodbye for the people involved. This may feel worse eventually for everyone. As with all things related to pet custody, it is important to check in with yourself to see if you are suggesting having the dogs visit each other is because you haven't yet come to terms with saying goodbye to your dog, or you might be looking for a reason to see your ex.

With repeated days apart, then time back together again, a dog may come to expect that his dog pal is coming home and might start showing behaviors like waiting at the door, listening for a certain car to pull up, or to look for their friend when the leash comes out. Especially for dogs who have a stronger connection to each other, a cycle of frequent reunions followed by long separations can be more worrying than doing it once.

To prepare a pair of dog friends to live without each other, I sug-gest having the dogs practice doing enjoyable activities away from each other with the guardian they will ultimately live with in the days or weeks leading up to their separation. By doing whatever brings your dog the most joy, such as training games, trips to the park, or even a simple walk around the neighborhood without the other dog, you will get them used to being in a happy state without their friend nearby.

This is a good time to use a Pheromone Collar for stress relief, to make sure your dog's routine is as familiar as possible, and to allow for an adjustment period while providing good enrichment, exercise and sufficient rest for your dog.

There are unavoidably challenging times during separations. Problems will arise. However, by thinking about things from your dog's perspective, you can minimize the length and intensity of the hard parts.

Summary questions

Are your dogs similar in energy levels, size and temperament?

How long have your dogs lived together?

Are the dogs genuinely attached to each other or do they just co-exist?

Chapter 9
Visitations

Jeremy and Jenny divorced after five years of marriage. They had a three-year-old chocolate Labrador. They agreed that Jenny would keep the dog, for several reasons but primarily because she was also keeping the house and she worked from home most of the time, while Jeremy was moving into a lock-up-and-go apartment and often travelled for work. They had a friendly rapport after the divorce, and Jenny invited Jeremy to visit Milo whenever he wanted. She didn't feel that it was fair for Jeremy and Milo never to see each other again.

A delightfully typical Labrador, Milo loved eating anything yummy and doing fun stuff. He was a well-adjusted and happy soul, enthusiastic about being a part of anything: going for walks, park runs or car drives; visiting coffee shops, dog friends and human friends; and playing fetch or participating in any sociable activity. His answer to everything was an eager, "YES!"

Initially, when Jeremy moved out, Milo seemed a little lost. Both he and Jenny had to navigate a stage of feeling sad and low. But Milo soon returned to his happy self and found a good groove again with Jenny.

Two weeks after moving out, Jeremy came around for his first visit. Milo was over the moon and unable to contain his excitement. From then on, depending on his work schedule, Jeremy would visit his pal Milo between once and three times a month. Occasionally twice in one week and then again only several weeks later.

During a typical visit, Jeremy would:

1. Take Milo to their favorite coffee shop for a *puppuccino* (an espresso cup filled with whipped cream).

2. Take Milo to the river for a swim.

3. Buy a hamburger, Milo's most fabulous meal to share with him.

4. Meet up with his friends and their dogs at the dog park, where dogs are allowed to run around without leads. Milo would play hard for another hour or so before heading back home to Jenny.

After Jeremy's visits, Milo started acting strange. For a few days after the visit, Milo would sleep at the door instead of in his bed. He would chew Jenny's furniture and howl when she left him at home alone. The tipping point for Jenny was when Milo ran away at the dog park. He had never done that before, and Jenny thought he'd run away to look for Jeremy. Jenny, realizing that she needed help, called me and asked whether Jeremy's visits were actually a good thing for Milo or not.

Visitations can be stressful for dogs

Here is the hard truth: Most dogs will end up more settled living with one guardian without visits from a previous guardian. Visitations are likely to be more distressing for your dog than comforting, even though they enjoy them at the time. Exhilaration followed by separation can create stress and anxiety for the dog. The dog constantly wonders, *Is today the day?* hoping their special person returns.

By stepping back into your dog's life only to leave him again, you may create more anxiety than happiness for him. You are recreating a situation in which they bond and separate repeatedly; reuniting for occasional visits forces them through an adjustment period of detachment every time. The visits themselves might be the most wonderful experience for your dog; it is the aftereffect that may be the most awful experience for them. For Milo, he was reunited with Jeremy... only to have him disappear again.

When a family splits up, people often can't help but think of their dogs as kids that they have the right to see. Children have the psychological need to stay in contact with their primary caregivers, but dogs do not have the same needs as children.

From a human perspective, it is fair for you to see your dog again. But from your dog's point of view, it would be better for you not to visit them.

In my many years of working with dogs who have been rehomed or adopted into a new family, I have observed that dogs adjust to new family settings more easily than you might imagine. When a dog moves into a new home, there certainly is a period of confusion and then they settle in with new people to love and a new routine to enjoy.

In situations where the decision to rehome a dog has been made, and finding them a suitable new home is best for all involved, I'm often asked, "Can we go and visit our dog even though they aren't ours anymore?" I have to say, "No, your dog can adjust into a new life after saying goodbye to you, but if you go back to see them, they will just be confused and feel left behind all over again."

There are of course exceptions. Possibilities vary according to the dogs and people involved. There are exes who visit their dogs without causing the dog or the people stress or heartache.

The key is to communicate honestly and openly about how the dog behaves after each visit. If you are the visitor and your ex says that the dog is unsettled and somewhat miserable after each visit, this could very well be the truth. Do you really want to insist on visiting if it stresses the dear dog when you go away again?

I never recommend having a video or phone call with a dog. It is a bad idea, especially if you have not seen them for a long time. When people call their dogs to talk to them, the poor dogs become frantic because they hear the voice but cannot smell or locate the actual person. It is easy to confuse stress with excitement in dogs. We are flooded by so called "cute" viral videos of dogs recognizing certain dog pals on video calls or their owner's voice over the phone, but when a dog can recognize a person on screen, they don't have the context to comprehend what is happening. The dog will try to locate the friend to greet them and of course cannot.

The desire to check on your dog after you have left is always a strong one. We would all want peace of mind knowing how your dog is doing once you have moved out, but seeing the dog for an hour won't really give you a clear indication of how the dog's day to day life is going. If you miss your dog and worry about them, ask if your ex will send you photos and video clips that can help to calm your fears.

Visitations, schedules and other tips

If you and your ex decide that you absolutely want visitations, here are recommendations to make it easier on your dog:

Keep the visits simple

Don't make up for lost time by overindulging your dog's appetite or doing every fun, high-energy thing they love. *This will create a deeper void and more disappointment for your dog when you leave.* Strange as it sounds, it is selfish to do too many wonderful things with your dog because their regular, ordinary life at home will be a lot less exciting in comparison. The dog will imagine that being with you would always be as exhilarating as it is when you visit, that you would always pay as much attention to them as you do then.

Choose one simple activity

While it isn't a good idea to overstimulate the dog, it is good for the visits to involve physical activity. This can help move the enthusiasm through the dog, rather than getting them overly excited. Get your dog moving with a walk and allow them to sniff and do normal doggy things, rather than just cuddling them indoors. Of course, if your dog cannot go outside for an adventure due to health or behavior problems, then stay in a location that is safe and comfortable for your dog.

Stay as relaxed as possible

Don't rev up your dog more than they will already be, especially when you first arrive. Pet them slowly and keep your voice calm. Do your best to remain collected and composed; don't cry or become overly demonstrative. Big emotions of any kind will worry your dog more than anything.

Try your best to stick to a regular schedule

For example, visit every Saturday, or every second Tuesday. Dogs eventually tune into the rhythm and will be less likely to perpetually expect visits.

We found a solution for Milo the Labrador, Jenny and Jeremy that worked for everyone. Jeremy didn't want Milo to be stressed after their time together. He understood that by making up for lost time with super exciting visits, he was causing Milo to miss him even more when he left.

Jeremy kept his visits much calmer and did not take Milo for puppuccinos or hamburgers. As a Lab, food was paramount for Milo, and anticipating culinary pleasure added to his ecstasy every time he heard Jeremy arrive. A typical visit became a drive to the river where Milo could walk, swim and fetch, and he gave him only a few small, standard treats.

Jenny reported that the change in intensity levels of the visits, and the absence of fabulous food, helped Milo to calm down. After Jeremy dropped Milo back at home, he was happy to settle back into his routine and he became his happy-go-lucky self again.

Dogs visiting dogs

If there is more than one dog, and the people who separate agree to divide the pets between them, what then? In the previous chapter, we discussed how dogs within a household may bond with each other. While it may not be ideal, there are certainly situations when strongly bonded dogs will have to be separated from each other after a divorce. It is very hard for dogs who are separated to be brought together again for *play dates*. It's not something that I would recommend from the perspective of your dog. While the greeting the dogs have is a joy to watch, the aftereffects are hard on them.

As with all things connected with pet custody, you must ask yourself if it is really the desire to see your ex, keeps tabs on them, or not let that relationship come to an end is the deeper reason you may be insisting to see your dog, or suggesting the two dogs get together for a visit. For many people, the dog becomes a very easy excuse to stay in communication and connection with a partner they are not able to let go of.

Summary questions

If your dog takes days to recover after you reunite and say goodbye again, will you still want to visit?

Does a continued connection with your dog cause tension between you and your ex?

If you intend to keep seeing your dog, what can you do to keep visitations calm and routine?

Chapter 10
Your Dog and Your Children

When there are children involved, should the dog move with the same custody schedule as them? Does it make sense for the dog to go wherever the kids do? If you bought a dog for your child, does that mean that the dog has connected with the child as their person in the same was as you intended?

If we are looking at a custody plan from the point of view of doing the best thing for the dog, it's important to find out whether the dog is primarily bonded with the children or one of the parents. I know of many divorce attorneys who advertise that they always design custody plans so that the dog moves with the children between parents, automatically. From the eyes of a dog, this isn't fair. Each dog, and each family dynamic, is unique. It is important to understand how shared or sole custody will affect them.

You may have a child who, when she gets back from school, is followed around by the dog wherever they go. There are dogs who want to be involved in all the child's activities, who choose to sleep close to the child, spend time with them at any opportunity. But there are also dogs who don't enjoy spending time in the company of children as much we think they do. For some dogs, the energy of children is problematic, and they gravitate more to one of the adults at home. We need to find out how involved the kids are with the dog, not what they promised when asking for a dog in the first place.

There are parents who regard the dog as emotional support for their children during a divorce; the parents want the dog to move with the children so that the children feel supported. But what is good for the kids may not be good for the dog in the long term. Some dogs are naturally steadier and calmer around emotional people. Other dogs will become overwhelmed and reactive if they are constantly exposed to people who are upset, acting strange or angry, all things that can happen during a divorce. Even the most tolerant of dogs will show a change in their behavior if too much is expected of them. Dogs who have previously been mellow souls never bite out of the blue. There are always signs beforehand that may be ignored or misunderstood by the people around them.

Is your dog more connected with you, or your kids?

When discussing a dog's long-term well-being after a breakup, it is helpful to observe your dog as honestly as possible. Take a deep breath and try to look at your dog as if you are seeing him for the first time. What clues can you get from your dog to help you understand what is happening for them inside? If a dog is very connected with and bonded to the children, then moving with the children between parents can work well. If, however, the dog is not particularly attached to the kids, this can become stressful for them.

By watching how the dog behaves, you can establish if they are more bonded with the parents or the children in a family.

When the children are at home, does the dog choose to spend time with them? Specifically, does the dog regularly choose to nap near them during the day? At night, does the dog want to sleep close to the kids? You can tell who dogs feel the most comfortable with because they choose to rest next to them. A sleeping or resting dog is at their most vulnerable and wants to be near someone predictable and with whom they feel most at ease. Dogs who love kids want to be close to them.

In my own house, I have four dogs and one teenage daughter who lives at home. My daughter has a Poodle who is unquestionably her dog. Bear (a big-hearted Mini Poodle) loves to be with people and will sit at my feet whenever I am at my computer. However, once my daughter is home from school, I don't even see Bear, he follows her like a shadow and always wants to be in her company. My other three dogs always greet my daughter when she comes home and are happy for scratches from her, but they never seek her out for company or specific social interaction. The other dogs are totally connected with me and my husband. For example, in our household,

Bear has bonded with my daughter and would prefer to be where she is, regardless of who is home because he is solidly connected with her. The other dogs should not as they have not gravitated to her.

Another way to tell if the dog is attached to a child, or finds them too unpredictable, is to discern what the dog does when that child is upset, crying or feeling ill. Do they seek out the child and provide comfort, or do they dislike the high emotion and stay away from the child? Regardless of breed, some dogs naturally come to wipe away the children's tears, and others will avoid it at all cost. Observing this in your dog is not a judgement on their character as good or bad, it simply means you can see them for who they are in a clear and kind way.

There are, of course, children of different ages and temperaments. If you've got smaller, playful kids, does your dog try to join in their games? Dogs that usually move more happily with the children will enjoy the loudness and bustle of kids playing, yelling and running. When the energy and noise levels of small kids goes up, what does your dog do? Disappear or join the party?

Scheduling custody for dogs and children

Nikki and James had three children and a five-year-old German Shepherd named Nala. When they amicably divorced, Nikki kept the house and had primary custody of the children. There was no question that Nala would remain at home with Nikki and the children. For the dog, they assumed, nothing much had changed.

Except that after a couple of weeks, Nala started destroying the furniture. She tore the couches to pieces, scratched holes in the wooden floor, ripped out the hems of the curtains, shredded the garden— you name it, she did it. Initially, I was called in as a behaviorist, not as a custody mediator, because both Nikki and James were happy with Nala staying there but were concerned about her behavior.

It is unusual for dogs to start becoming destructive at five years old. Typically, this sort of behavior or habit starts in adolescent dogs. My curiosity was up when I got the call from Nikki about what was happening for Nala since she only started becoming destructive at her age. Once I had a history, I understood what had led to the change in Nala's behavior.

Prior to their divorce, James took Nala for a run every morning and played Frisbee with her at the park. So Nala got vigorous exercise on a daily basis. The run and playing games appeared to tire Nala out because when she returned home, she would sleep much of the day until the kids came home. Nikki did not have the time to take Nala out every day as her time was full caring for her three kids. Some days the children would go to the park after school with Nala, but the walk was a mellow one and not regular. Nala suddenly lost her daily exercise, the outlet for her energy levels and desire to work; in her case her "job" was her morning run and frisbee time. Nala loved the children, but the primary factor that was going to keep her happy was regular exercise and activity. There was no deeper, philosophical, psychological reason for her destructive behavior other than boredom and frustration about no exercise.

I spoke with the whole family and suggested that James keep Nala for a month, to see if her behavior would improve. The children would see her on the weekends and every other Wednesday which is when they were scheduled to visit their dad. James lived in a smaller house and there wasn't a big yard for Nala to run around in; and yet she improved. She slept soundly and was completely peaceful, thanks to her run and fun with the Frisbee every morning.

I return to this story often because, honestly, dog behavior we call "bad" happens when they appear to be frustrated and bored. Without enough outlets for all the energy they have stored in their bodies, they start to bark, chew, dig, and so on.

When families are planning on life post-divorce with their dog, we have to look at the exercise needs of the dog and whether or not the dog will still get the time they need to be happy and content with a change in lifestyle.

If the dog is used to two walks a week and they're fine with that, you have less to worry about. But if the dog is used to several walks a day, they're still going to need to have several walks a day.

I do find that it is better for an even tempered, happy, mellow dog to move with the children than without them; the kids provide some continuity, and they can fall into the routine of accompanying the children. But, if having the children prevents the parents from exercising the dog, managing any behavior concerns, or if the dog is much more attached to one parent than anyone else, it would be better to have the dog live with one parent and see the kids part-time.

Summary questions

Does your dog choose to lay next to your kids when they are resting or do they prefer to lay next to you?

Does your dog get involved in the children's activities, or do they seem to have less energy than the children?

Are you able to keep up with your dog's exercise and enrichment needs when you have the children with you?

Chapter 11
Coming to Grips with
Your Decision

Your dog does not ruminate on the hardships of the past, and this is a good lesson for us too. Practice mindfulness and gratitude and you will better understand how your dog thinks and feels. Learn from your dog how to live in the moment. Your dog wants nothing more than joy and contentment. And a good squirrel to chase.

Parting ways

I've said it before and say it again: Shared custody is rarely the best option for the dog. If a dog can tolerate shared custody, it's the guardians who are the lucky ones, not the dog.

Even if you think that you can offer your dog a better life than your ex, but they legally own the dog or fight you for custody, it can be wiser to let the dog go to them than insist on shared custody. A consistent life with one custodian can be better for a dog than having to share it when two people can't stop fighting over them.

Sometimes, a person may feel an increase in devotion to their dog during or after a divorce. It can seem as if the dog offers a chance at redemption, for a person to prove that they are lovable and can see a relationship through to the end. They may feel, without realizing it, that being a successful dog person will make up for the failure of their human relationship. It may seem as if the dog is all they have left. As if it's them and their dog against the world. They may want to provide the perfect conditions for their pet, to be the perfect pet owner. But all of this is about them, not the dog.

A dog whose owners divorce can get used to living without one of them quicker than you may think. Dogs love reunions and the excitement of greeting someone familiar, but their eagerness should not be taken to mean that they sit and miss those people beforehand.

Dogs say goodbye a lot easier than people do. They don't pine for people. People don't always want to hear this because we want our dogs to need us.

If you don't get custody of the dog or decide that the dog would be better off with your ex, you will have to be mature and brave about saying a proper goodbye. Your heart may feel as if it is breaking, but your dog will be okay.

When you say goodbye, do it knowing that you will not see the dog again because this is what is best for the dog. Make it a memorable parting by spending time alone with the dog, grateful to them for all they have brought to your life. Accept the pain of parting and be kind to yourself. Ask a friend to support you afterward, and don't expect too much of yourself for a while.

An old lady once said that growing old is all about loss. "You lose your youth, your agility, your eyesight, your hearing and your loved ones." Then she smiled, saying, "As long as you can adapt, you'll be just fine."

Although there is much loss throughout one's life, there is also great gain. With the loss of youth, comes the gain of experience; with physical loss there comes the gain of wisdom; and with the loss of loved ones there comes the gain of becoming centered in oneself rather than others.

Is rehoming an option?

Two of my clients, Angelo and Mark, found themselves in this predicament, made more complicated by the fact that there were two dogs involved. Initially, they agreed to share custody. But Mark met someone new, started commuting from upstate to downstate, and couldn't take both dogs on the plane or drive them for eight hours in the car every weekend. His new partner didn't want the dogs at all. Angelo, in the meantime, said that he couldn't take both dogs because it was too expensive, and he lived in a studio. He also couldn't travel with both dogs, but he could put one in his backpack and ride with on his bicycle. They discussed the possibility of each taking one dog or contributing financially to the upkeep of both dogs in one home, but they became stuck there. One dog was four and the other six; they were both rescues, and neither was overly bonded to one or the other of them. Although Mark seemed to want to keep a dog, or both dogs, if need be, his lifestyle and new partner did not support it. In this case, rehoming was the wisest decision. The dogs did not need to be caught up in the fine details and personal preferences of owners to whom they were not much attached.

While it is rare to rehome a dog to the home of someone other than the owners or to a shelter or breed rescue organization, deciding to rehome a dog is not a sin. Dogs will always be happiest in a home where they are wanted, and the people have the time and energy to give the dogs what they need. If you are in this situation, ask for help from professionals who have the resources available to help you find an appropriate, loving home for your dog.

Anyone who judges you for rehoming, or immigrating without your dogs, has likely never been in a situation like yours. There are times when people think that they love their dogs but treat them more like objects or symbols of a settled life when they are anything but settled.

I believe we should love all dogs enough to make sure they are in the best home possible, even if that is with a different family.

Getting a new dog

Although there is loss, there is plenty of opportunity for new beginnings.

Even if saying goodbye is an experience you think that you can never go through again, you do not have to live without a dog. In the same way that you looked ahead when considering what was best for the dog from whom you have parted, you can look ahead to a better future for yourself, too. When you are ready, you can think about getting another dog or pet. There are so many other animals out there in need of a loving home.

Perhaps it was a mere coincidence that you ended up with the dog you had; perhaps it was destiny. You have the benefit of experience now. You understand more about dogs and what the breeds are like, whether the breed of dog you had is the kind of dog you are most compatible with, and what kind of dog will suit your new life. Would a puppy do well with you, or would you prefer an adult?

If you have read this book to discover the right decision for your dog's sake and have honestly answered at least a few of the questions at the end of every chapter, I am sure that you will be able to make the choices that your dog needs you to make.

Summary questions

How can you come to terms with saying goodbye?

Do you have the place in your heart for another pet?

If so, could you use the opportunity to adopt a puppy or adult dog from an animal welfare organization?

Chapter 12
When and Where to Get
Professional Help

Before we discuss when to get professional help, it's important to define what *professional* means in the dog training and behavior industry.

A dog trainer is a person who teaches dogs, from the basics at puppy school to advanced obedience for service dogs or search-and-rescue dogs and everything in between. The term behaviorist or behavior consultant, is reserved for someone with higher qualifications than a trainer; the behaviorist has learned how to deal with dogs with problems such as anxiety, aggression and all manner of serious issues. They are experts in behavior modification and can identify why a dog is having behavior issues and provide owners with a specific plan to improve it.

Look for certified professionals

There are credible, regulated bodies and associations that appropriately certify and monitor people who work with animals, with a standard of knowledge and a code of ethics. It is crucial that you find a qualified professional whenever you need help or advice about your dog's behavior, and especially in hard situation like going through divorce.

The International Association of Animal Behavior Consultants, the Animal Behavior Society and the Certification Council of Professional Dog Trainers are the largest and most credible international certifying bodies for dog behavior experts. Look for a certified dog behavior consultant (CDBC, CBCC-KA), Certified applied animal behaviorist (CAAB) or certified professional dog trainer (CPDT-KA) or equivalent qualification. They will have years of extensive experience, educational requirements and will have passed rigorous tests to have these titles. In other words, these qualifications can't be bought, they must be earned! Visit www.iaabc.org or www.ccpdt.org to find a consultant near you.

In addition, you can go to my website (whokeepsthedog.com) for a link to a list of certified dog professionals who have completed my Certified Pet Custody Consultant course. I created a course specifically to teach dog experts how to assist their clients when going through a divorce.

A word of caution

Unfortunately, the dog training and behavior industry is not regulated, and the titles of "dog trainer" or "dog behaviorist" are not legal terms. Anyone can print business cards describing themselves as an animal expert of some kind, and there's nothing that anyone can do to stop them. Or people can spend $20 on an online course and receive a certificate claiming that they are qualified dog specialists of some sort. I have met many so-called certified behaviorists who have made situations much worse and have caused trauma to dogs and people because they didn't have the education or experience to appropriately work with challenging cases.

If someone cannot provide proof of qualifications, or just says they are certified to work with animals, this is not someone you should involve with a pet custody matter. Qualified professionals should show you letters of recommendation from vets, colleagues and other clients they work with if you ask for them.

In a child custody case, only a social worker or child psychologist would be called on to make recommendations about a child's well-being. Likewise, only a qualified behaviorist should be consulted about a pet custody case. If you end up in court, you'll certainly need your dog experts to have qualifications to be taken seriously. But even in mediation, make sure that you obtain proof of qualifications and letters of recommendation.

Where to begin your search

In addition to the websites mentioned above, ask trusted dog professionals in your area for recommendations for qualified and experienced behavior professionals. Your regular vet can be used to discuss your dog's medical needs, but unless they are a specialized veterinary behaviorist, they are unlikely to have the background in dog behavior that is necessary in custody discussions. Ask your vet, rescue groups, shelters, breeders or groomers in your area if they have a recommendation for a qualified dog professional to whom they refer behavior cases.

When should you find an expert?

If you and your ex can't agree about your dog's stress levels during a shared custody trial period, it is time to get professional help. You might not think the dog is stressed or that you need expert advice, but if you start fighting over the dog without resolving the issue, a professional can help you to do what is best for the dog. One of you might say, "Rover's not stressed at all!" while the other insists, "Rover is stressed!"

In addition, don't be shy to reach out and ask for help to make sure your dog is adjusting to any routine changes as best as possible. I remember one recently-separated woman whose dog was showing signs of separation anxiety after she had moved to a new home and her dog no longer was spending his days with her work-from-home ex-husband. After giving her a practical and helpful plan to resolve the issue, she was so grateful. She said with all the changes she was going through she was so relieved for someone to tell her what to do so she didn't have to figure everything out herself!

If you are unsure as to why your dog is acting in a certain way, or if you are making assumptions about why your dog is behaving out of character, don't be too shy to reach out to an expert!

Chapter 13
"Dear Guardian"

Here is the kind of letter I imagine that your dog would write to you, if they could, at this moment in your life.

Dear Guardians,

Life is changing for all of us now.

You and my other guardian are not together anymore, and I'm cool with that if you are. I can tell it's been hard on you, but you are brave, and I believe in you.

Sometimes I thought that you were trying to growl and bark at one another. Your language is pretty complicated. Sometimes I was scared and confused.

But I don't hold it against you. I don't dwell on bad things from the past; I remember the good things and expect them to happen again, so I'm very optimistic about the future. Mostly, though, I just like to live in the present. Especially if it involves a bone to chew on, a walk, a bowl of fresh water, a sleep in my favorite spot or an affectionate rub.

Thank you for your promise to put aside your emotions that might prevent you from making the best decision about me. You and my other guardian know me better than anyone else so I'm glad it's you trying to make a decision. I'm grateful to you for trying to keep your conversations about me on topic. I'm also thankful to you for treating me like the dog that I am rather than like a child.

It's okay if you forget and make mistakes along the way. I know that you will make a good choice on my behalf because you love me.

I will adjust to new circumstances. If you try to share me between homes, and I can't take it, I trust that you will notice and let me stay in one place. Some dogs just want to stay where they are, without dividing themselves between people.

If we have to say goodbye, I may be confused at first but don't worry about me. I will continue to be positive and enthusiastic about life.

Thank you for loving me enough to make the best plan for me that you can.

Yours Gratefully,

Rover

Chapter 14
For Dog Professionals

To anyone who works with dogs professionally: veterinarians, dog trainers, groomers, breeders, dog walkers, pet sitters, behavior consultants, or volunteers at shelters or rescue groups, this chapter is for you. If you haven't yet encountered one of your clients going through a breakup or divorce, it is only a matter of time. If you work at a shelter, you have likely encountered people surrendering their animals because of a divorce when their circumstances left them no other choice. Many vets I know have been in an awful position when they found out that a dog they put to sleep was done to hurt a person's ex by lying to the vet that the dog had become dangerous in some way and needed to be put down.

Talk to new owners about the ramifications of a breakup

As professionals who spend their time with people who may have just bought or adopted a new dog or pup, I implore you to start incorporating into your conversations with new dog owners the question of who will keep the dog in the unlikely event of a breakup. A petnup is a wonderful way to do this. There are various forms available online, from my website as well as other places. My wish is for it to become standard practice that all adoption centers, breed rescue groups, humane organizations and breeders have owners fill in a petnup as standard practice anytime a new dog is brought home. This would save countless hours of potential heartache, confusion, money, and stress for both the people and the dog.

When your clients tell you they are getting a divorce and they already have a dog, they may be at a loss as to what to do. From the behavior side of the equation, remind them to be consistent about exercise and enrichment to help the dog better deal with the inevitably more stressful household. Given the breed of dog and what you know of the personality of the owner, give them as many practical ideas as possible, but not so many that they feel overwhelmed. Sometimes some extra help, like hiring a dog walker or asking friends to take the dog to the park, can be a huge relief for people.

Sadly, divorce can bring out the worst in people. While this book is directed towards people who would consider mediation an option, that is certainly not the case for everyone. Several times each week, I hear from someone whose ex-partner went to their house, before the locks got changed, took the dog and simply disappeared. If, for lack of a better word, things have gotten ugly between your client and their ex, I would recommend they immediately get legal advice and make sure the dog is in a safe place.

Make sure you keep good records

If you run a dog daycare, kennel, grooming parlor or anywhere else that a dog may be left with you, make sure it is always clear in your records which people are allowed to pick up the dog. Anytime a client tells you they are in the middle of a breakup, be sure you have the difficult conversation about who is allowed to take the dog home. It is also sadly very common, during a contentious divorce, that a dog is picked up at dog daycare, and then a letter from that person's lawyer is delivered stating that they are suing for custody, and it can be months of legal battles before the situation is resolved, if ever.

Tell clients about mediation services

When clients are having an amicable divorce or breakup, they may tell you they and their ex are simply going to share their dog, that there are no ill feelings between them. This is the ideal time to suggest mediation to them, to help them come up with a plan and contract that will work for both. Even the friendliest of breakups can turn very sour after some months or years of sharing a dog, and then it is infinitely harder to be patient and reasonable with each other. As I said earlier in this book, the sooner things are resolved about the dog, the better. It is not enough to have a conversation about it. People need a clear, written contract, without any ambiguities as to the meaning or intentions behind it. Mediation is the most cost-effective, peaceful and empowering way to do this.

If you, as a dog professional, would like to work directly with people navigating pet custody, read the next chapter on how to become a pet custody consultant.

Chapter 15
How to Work with Pet
Custody Clients

I have a dream that one day education about ethical, animal-focused pet custody practices will be part of the training and instruction for all divorce lawyers and mediators.

Professional development opportunities

To that end, the part of my work I am most proud of is my development of the first pet custody courses for both divorce and dog professionals. The students in the two courses are different: one is designed to teach divorce experts about *dogs*; the other teaches dog experts about *divorce*. However the goal is the same, whatever your background, you will learn best practices for pets involved in a custody situation.

My greatest passion and joy are sharing what I know about dogs, and people, with others. In developing these courses, I distilled the essence of my almost 30 years of experience working with dogs and their people, my years as a family mediator, as a twice-divorced mother, conversations with countless law professionals and people going through divorce with pets. I have presented my courses and workshops for a variety of institutions including the American Bar Association, The Kentucky Bar Association, The Association of Family Mediators, International Mediation Week, The Ontario Association of Family Mediators, and The South African Association of Mediators. In addition, I have been invited to speak at many mediation conferences around the world in India, Ireland, Australia, Canada, the United Kingdom, South Africa and the USA.

If you are a lawyer, mediator or anyone who works in the arena of divorce and this book has inspired you to learn more about the topic of pet custody, my course is for you. If many of your existing clients have dogs and you haven't been too sure what the best path forward is, my course is for you. Or if you would like to specialize in pet custody, helping people during a pet custody, with divorcing or separating couples, to help ensure that the custody decision they make looks after the needs of the pets, then, you guessed it, my course is for you! For more information see my website at www.whokeepsthedog.com.

Certification opportunities

For the dog professionals who attend my course, you can empower yourself with a unique skill set as a Certified Pet Custody Consultant. Here you will learn to work with your own clients as well as in collaboration with divorce professionals in your area as a consultant for pet custody issues. My course is open to qualified dog professionals who have a capacity for working with people navigating difficult emotions and challenging situations and is approved by both the IAABC and CCPDT for CEUs.

For more information, or to apply for an upcoming course, visit www.whokeepsthedog.com.

Recommended Reading
and Other Resources

Canine Enrichment for the Real World by Allie Bender and Emily Strong. Dogwise Publishing, 2019.

Mood Matters by Karin Pienaar. Dogwise Publishing, 2022.

The Stress Factor in Dogs by Kristina Spaulding. Dogwise Publishing, 2022.

On Tallking Terms With Dogs by Turid Rugass. Dogwise Publishing, 2005.

Assessing Aggression Thresholds in Dogs by Sue Sternberg. Dogwise Publishing, 2016.

Meet Your Dog by Kim Brophey. Chronicle Books, 2018.

Resources

Food puzzle toys

Karis Nafte website www.whokeepsthe dog.com

Pheromone collars

   https://thundershirt.com/

   https://www.adaptil.com/us

Trainer/Behavior help:

   IAABC: https://iaabc.org/

   Animal Behavior Society: https://www.animalbehaviorsociety.org/

   CCPDT: https://www.ccpdt.org/

About the Author

Karis Nafte, CDBC, has a special set of skills; the combination of being a dog behavior expert and a divorce mediator gives Karis a unique perspective into the world of dogs and divorce. Her pioneering pet custody work as the first person to address divorce as to its effects on dogs, has created the foundation, and focus, of her business *Who Keeps the Dog*.

A speaker for the American Bar Association, the Kentucy Bar Association, the South African Association of Mediators, the Association for Professional Family Mediators, and International Mediation Week, her work with pet custody has also been featured in *ABC News, Vice News, Australian Dog Lovers Magazine, The Daily Telegraph, Pets Lifestyle Magazine, The New York Post, Scripps News, the Associated Press, the Arkansas Law Review,* and the *International Association of Animal Behavior Consultants Journal.*

Her qualification as a Certified Dog Behavior Consultant (CDBC) is through the International Association for Animal Behavior Consultants. The IAABC is the worldwide benchmark organization for certified professionals in animal behavior work; their certifications are the most rigorous in the field of animal behavior and training. The qualification of a CDBC is only granted to professionals who have the experience and knowledge to work effectively, and humanely, with the most challenging of dog behavior cases. As an Internationally Accredited Family Law Mediator, Karis works worldwide with couples getting divorced, or anyone in positions of conflict who choose a neutral mediator to facilitate a resolution instead of going to court.

In addition to her work with private clients, she teaches internationally to divorce mediators and lawyers who want to learn best practice for handling pet custody cases.

Karis has been working professionally with dogs since 1997. During her career, she has worked with thousands of different dogs and owners and has well over 30,000 hours of experience both training dogs and providing behavior consultations. Karis can be reached through her website at www.whokeepsthedog.com.

Did you enjoy this book?

WRITE A REVIEW!

REVIEWS HELP OTHER READERS DECIDE ON THEIR NEXT BOOK! GO TO WWW.DOGWISE.COM AND SELECT A STAR RATING (1-5) THEN LEAVE SOME COMMENTS DESCRIBING WHAT YOU ENJOYED OR SOMETHING YOU LEARNED WHILE READING THIS BOOK!

Write a Review   ✕

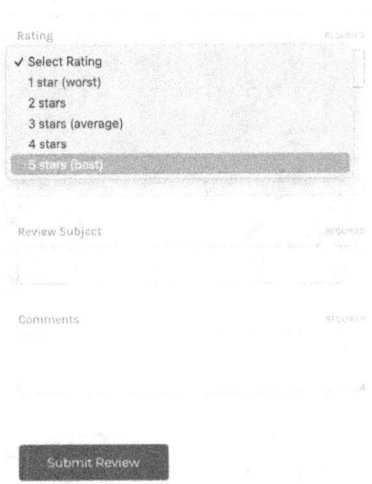

All things dog.

Dogwise™
All things dog.

Connect with us

FOLLOW, LIKE, AND TAG US ON SOCIAL MEDIA TO STAY CONNECTED

SCAN THE QR CODES BELOW WITH YOUR PHONE'S CAMERA APP TO GO DIRECTLY TO OUR SOCIAL MEDIA PROFILES

instagram
@dogwise.books

facebook
/dogwise

twitter
@DogwiseBooks

www.ingramcontent.com/pod-product-compliance
Lightning Source LLC
Chambersburg PA
CBHW071211280526
45787CB00002B/647